A COMMON SENSE GUIDE TO WORLD PEACE

By
BENJAMIN B. FERENCZ

Introduction by
LOUIS B. SOHN
Bemis Professor of International Law
Harvard Law School, Emeritus
Woodruff Professor of International Law
University of Georgia School of Law

OCEANA PUBLICATIONS, INC.
LONDON • ROME • NEW YORK

ABOUT THE AUTHOR

Benjamin B. Ferencz has dedicated a good portion of his life to seeking a just and tranquil international society where all may live in peace and dignity regardless of their race or creed.

A graduate of the Harvard Law School, Dr. Ferencz saw active military service in World War II, where he participated in the liberation of several Nazi concentration camps. At the age of 27, he became the Chief Prosecutor for the United States in the Nuremberg war crimes trial against German extermination squads that had murdered over a million innocent people. He forged legal precedents regarding crimes against humanity. As the Director of post-war restitution programs, he helped to fashion and implement new laws to compensate survivors of Nazi persecution. He practiced international law in New York and was elected a Vice-President of the American Society of International Law. He is an accredited non-governmental observer at the United Nations.

He is the author of many articles and of several books, including the prize-winning *Less Than Slaves* (Harvard University Press, 1979) that was made into a television documentary. He is active in several peace societies and is a frequent lecturer. As an Adjunct Professor of International Law at Pace University, Dr. Ferencz teaches "The International Law of Peace." He is married, has four grown children, and lives in New Rochelle, New York.

OTHER BOOKS BY BENJAMIN B. FERENCZ

Defining International Aggression - The Search for World Peace: A Documentary History and Analysis. 2 volumes. New York: Oceana Publications, Inc., 1975.

Less Than Slaves: Jewish Forced Labor and the Quest for Compensation. Cambridge, Massachusetts and London: Harvard University Press, 1979. German Edition: *Lohn Des Grauens* (Campus Verlag, Frankfurt).

An International Criminal Court - A Step Toward World Peace: A Documentary History and Analysis. 2 volumes. New York: Oceana Publications, Inc., 1980.

Enforcing International Law - A Way to World Peace: A Documentary History and Analysis. 2 volumes. New York: Oceana Publications, Inc., 1983.

Library of Congress Catalog Card Number: 85-40756
ISBN: 0-379-20797-4

Manufactured in the United States of America

This book is respectfully dedicated to those leaders of the United States and the Soviet Union who will have the courage and the wisdom to overcome their fears and reconcile their differences, so that all who dwell on this planet may live together in peace and dignity regardless of their race or creed.

TABLE OF CONTENTS

PART THREE: WHAT *CAN* BE DONE

INTRODUCTION

In days of gloom and prophets of doom, it is good to have before us a book that is optimistic, if only "cautiously optimistic," the author claiming that he is presenting to us a glass "half-full rather than half-empty."

The author first paints an impressionistic picture of that half-full glass showing what has been done to develop rules of international law, procedures for settling international disputes, and institutions for enforcing these rules and dispute-settling decisions. In the second part of the book, the author describes colorfully the elixirs that are needed to brim the glass of peace—what *should* be done to bring peace to the world. The third part explores what *can* realistically be done in view of the formidable obstacles that must be overcome.

In Part I, the author summarizes succinctly the accomplishments of the last 4,000 years and, in particular, the results of the accelerated pace of the forty years since World War II. While newspapers, television and other media record in detail the catastrophies, the wars, the revolutions, the famines and other disasters that constantly befall mankind, only a few experts note: That in those forty years more international agreements have been concluded than during the previous four milennia; that the International Court of Justice after a period of unemployment has now more cases than it can comfortably handle (including several cases testifying to its acceptance by the African countries and other new members of the international community); that several regional and functional courts are dealing with a rapidly increasing number of cases; and that more than two hundred international organizations deal with matters of daily concern to the majority of mankind in such an efficient and smooth way that their activities are generally accepted without a murmur.

The author is rightly not satisfied with all these positive developments, as they are lost in the waves of negative thinking. A lot more needs to be done to enable the joint efforts of enlightened humanity to prevail over the obstacles posed by obsolete traditions, narrow concepts of national interest, and unwillingness to adapt to the novel conditions of the nuclear age.

Parts II and III are interconnected. They are less historical, more prescriptive. The author shows how international law can be improved by drafting new codes that would reflect "greater tolerance and compassion for sincere differences in perspective regarding what is required for the wellbeing of all peoples." Instead of indulging in the proclamation of such abstract principles as self-determination, non-interference in international affairs, or non-use of force, it is necessary to eliminate legal loopholes, in particular by spelling out in advance and in sufficient detail the conditions for applying these principles and the unavoidable exceptions. The author points out also that principles need to be flexible and easily adjustable, as "no rights can be considered immutable and absolute; they are subject to change and must be weighed against other rights."

Such rules will not help, however, if national decision-makers should continue to arrogate to themselves the right to determine in each case whether the rules permit them to engage in a particular activity regardless of consequences to other countries. This kind of traditional self-judging privilege has to be replaced by conferring on impartial international tribunals or boards the power to decide whether a particular activity is legal; what are the bounds for that activity, and what correlative restrictions should be imposed on other parties to avoid unnecessary provocation. All disputes should be settled "legally, not lethally" as escalation of any dispute may provoke the participation of superpowers. Any dispute can endanger the future of mankind and the life on our planet. The Charter of the United Nations is correct in emphasizing that any dispute or situation, "the continuance of which is likely to endanger the maintenance of international peace and security," is of concern to the United Nations as a whole. While some peace violations may be dealt with by ordinary means at the disposal of the United Nations, the author would like to see an international criminal court with jurisdiciton over most grievous offenses against the peace and security of mankind.

Both national and international experiences show that most rules are obeyed by most individuals and states most of the time simply as a matter of convenience, routine and reciprocity. Nevertheless, occasional violators need to be stopped and, if necessary, punished. The attempts to endow the United Nations with powers required for this purpose have proved fruitless. The rights of five permanent members of the Security Council to veto any enforcement decision protects not only them but also their friends. Other countries feel that it would be unfair and inequitable to enforce the law against only those countries who cannot count on such a veto.

In addition, as long as nations are heavily armed, no international peacekeeping force can be strong enough to maintain international peace, except perhaps against some ministates, and only if no major power objects. Only if national arms should be sufficiently reduced would an international force become meaningful. The author would start by cutting down nuclear arsenals but admits that conventional arms must also be cut drastically before an international force would be able to disarm persistent belligerents and maintain peace.

The author also believes that we cannot have peace in an unjust world as injustice, sooner or later, leads to conflict and even internal oppression may lead to international involvement. "When the misuse of others is ignored or accepted, it threatens us all." The only possible solution is to "increase sharing and caring."

To find a way out of our morass the author recommends the creation of a Permanent Council of Peace which would replace the many commissions that in recent years have tried to cope with the complex problems faced by the world community. It would be composed of "renowned thinkers, spiritual, community and business leaders," free of the ideological biases that block solutions to many international problems. Its task would be to mobilize world opinion by disseminating its proposals "through all of the modern means of communication as well as through the many institutions dedicated to a tranquil world." He believes that a "determined international campaign of truth and wisdom led by a Council of dedicated, knowledgeable and distinguished world citizens could go over the heads of governments to reach the eyes, ears, hearts and minds of people everywhere."

Pending the establishment of that Council, the best thing we could do is to read this book carefully and encourage others to read it. It is a real "common sense guide to world peace."

LOUIS B. SOHN
Bemis Professor of International Law,
Emeritus
Harvard Law School

Woodruff Professor of International Law
University of Georgia School of Law

Athens, Georgia, August, 1985

PREFACE

For the first time in history, it lies within man's power to destroy all life on earth. National and economic rivalries, competing political ideologies and contemporary outbursts of racial and religious intolerance lacerate the fabric of international society. Unless change by non-violent means is made possible, change by violent means becomes inevitable. If peoples of differing persuasion cannot learn to live together in peace, they will probably die together in war. It is reasonable to assume, however, that the mortal mind which was able to invent devices powerful enough to threaten world survival is also capable of devising measures to prevent the immolation of civilization. Means must be found which will make it possible for differences to be respected without jeopardizing the security of humankind. How this can and must be done is the subject of this book.

To begin with, I ask the reader to approach the topic with an open mind. The belief that intractable problems are best left to experts or government leaders, may prove to be a fatal assumption. Professional diplomats and elected officials who are paid to protect a parochial interest can hardly be expected to favor innovations that may entail sacrifices by their constituents; the common sense of the common man may prove to be a better protector of the common weal.

It is a conviction widely held, particularly in the United States, that with sufficient determination and application, all problems can be resolved in a fairly brief period of time. The enormous strides made on the American continent since 1776, the landing of American astronauts on the previously unreachable moon, and the nearly unimaginable feats of modern technology all lend credence to this pervasive sense of human invincibility. Despite such feelings of euphoria, no one should expect quick or easy solutions to problems that have plagued mankind for centuries. But I shall offer a frame of reference which I hope will stimulate thought and thereby help to illuminate the path to future peace. My approach is a cautiously optimistic one; both as a matter of principle and because I believe it is justified by the facts. Without faith that human betterment is possible, despondency would stifle the initiative required to avert the prophecies of doom. Hope is the motor that drives human endeavor and only through confidence in the future can humankind muster the courage and strength to do what is required for survival. With all due respect to those of contrary opinion, I have therefore, deliberately chosen to view the historical glass as half-full rather than half-empty.

It is my contention that — despite all of the vicissitudes and strife —an objective analysis of the facts will show that humankind is experiencing an erratic and turbulent evolutionary movement toward a more rational world order. I shall point out some of the landmarks along the historical road to demonstrate that more progress has been made during the past four decades than in all of previous recorded history. Only in fairly recent times have people begun to understand the interdependence, complexity and fragility of life on this planet. New organizations and instrumentalities are being created and improved in an effort to enhance the quality of life everywhere. There has been a gradual awakening of the universal human conscience. I do not mean to suggest that improvements in the human condition are inevitable — quite the contrary — but awareness that changes for the better are taking place, and the ability to see the wavering line of progress, should lend encouragement to those who are determined to make such advances even more effective. These new-born creations are frail babes that must be nurtured with loving care if they are to reach maturity and play their proper role in an enlightened world. We must not be tempted to abandon a babe just because it was not born full-grown.

In order to understand the action that is required now, it is important to master the lessons of history. Misinterpreting the past leads to misunderstanding the present and misjudging the future. There are those who will point out that ever since man began to roam this earth, he has never managed to eliminate the terrible evil of war as a means of settling disputes. They may argue that the historical record proves that killing other human beings is an immutable characteristic of man's nature and that all efforts to curb this natural destructive tendency are futile. I am not inclined to accept this melancholy Hobbesian theory of inherent human brutality. I do not believe that we are all fore-doomed to share the fate of the dinosaur. The human instinct for survival, coupled with the intellect that distinguishes man from beast has, thus far, intervened to protect humankind from extinction. Despite lapses and regressions, we can learn, and are learning, from errors of the past. There is nothing inevitable about either war or peace; whether we survive or not depends on us.

The harsh reality we face is that close to five billion people of vastly different cultures and values — of varied national, religious, racial and ethnic attachments — now inhabit one planet and compete for its benefits and blessings. A few have great wealth, while hundreds of million suffer hunger or malnutrition. Some nations have great strength, others are weak. Tyranny and fear dominate large masses. National pride swells in the hearts of newly independent nations, while self-determination remains an unfulfilled dream of oppressed minorities in all parts of the globe. By fair means or foul, hostile political and religious ideologies vie for acceptance and power. Acts that are condemned as illegal aggressions by some are hailed as wars of liberation by others. One group's terrorism is another's heroism. The challenge we confront is whether we can subdue this explosive mélange long enough to fashion the conditions needed for a peaceful world. Perfect solutions should not be expected; it is inevitable that conflicts will continue to arise, just as they do within many families and inside the most orderly of nations. The fact that remedies are less than perfect does not mean that the search for improvements should be abandoned; to do so would invite consequences that would be infinitely more disastrous. Though the situation is fraught with peril, it is far from hopeless. The eager and discerning eye can find, in the lessons of the past and the needs of the present, new policies that can help guide us out of our dangerous morass.

In our search for the path to world peace, it may be simple common sense to focus on what has already been universally accepted as the essential structure for all orderly societies. Since ancient times, every village, town, city and nation-state has come to recognize that a peaceful domestic society requires: 1) laws (to specify what may or may not be done), 2) courts (to resolve disputes and decide whether the codes have been violated), and 3) a system of effective law enforcement. To the extent that these three conditions are met, there is relative tranquility; to the extent that they are absent, there is turmoil. In the much more heterogeneous and complicated international arena, we find, unfortunately, that laws are inadequate, courts lack binding authority and enforcement is practically nonexistent. Small wonder that upon taking office in 1982, U.N. Secretary-General, Javier Perez de Cuellar, referred to the "prevailing international anarchy." But this grim picture is not quite as bleak as may appear on the surface. I shall explore the developments in each of these three vital areas to show what has been accomplished and what still needs to be done.

My thesis, simply stated, is that the arch or bridge to peace consists of these three major interlocking components — law, courts and enforcement — but they must all be set in place before the structure can be expected to stand. The foundation-stone of law remains barren without courts, and courts remain ineffective without enforcement. Each part is connected and depends upon the other for support. But the problem is even more complex; each major buttress also requires additional reinforcing elements. Thus, before international law can become more meaningful, there must be greater clarification and acceptance of the norms which are to govern international behavior. This, in turn, requires more universally shared values, mutual trust or confidence and a willingness to reach agreement through compromise. Until there is general consent to codifying the basic minimum norms of international behavior, one cannot realistically expect broad acceptance of independent courts to interpret those standards — or the granting of power to any independent agency to enforce rules of national conduct. Before international courts can become more acceptable, there must also be increased respect for the judicial process itself and greater willingness to rely on courts rather than on arms to resolve international disputes. If international law enforcement is to become a reality, the United Nations Organization and similar organs for international cooperation must be improved. Nations cannot be allowed to decide for themselves when they will use armed force to protect their interests. National arms must be brought under international controls and self-help through warlike action must be replaced by a system of coordinated economic or military sanctions supported by the overwhelming might of the world community. An International Peace Force must be created as the ultimate international law enforcement agency. Those who are expected to comply with such a design for international law and order must be convinced that the proclaimed standards are as fair as can be expected under the circumstances and that the objective of the system is not exploitation but social justice for the betterment of all of humankind. Each supporting component of the structure depends upon the other. The coherent and cohesive plan produces a strengthened or synergistic effect. If essential parts of the edifice are lacking, the structure is in danger of collapse.

The most immediate and compelling requirement is for a drastic reduction in the nuclear weapons that pose an impending threat to civilization. If the human house is undermined and faces a risk of imminent explosion, it is common sense that defusing the hazard must be given top priority. The most impressive blueprint for an improved society of nations would become meaningless if widespread nuclear warfare should destroy all of humankind. Arms control and disarmament are urgently imperative for other reasons as well; budgetary deficits, caused primarily by the enormous expense of preparing for war, pose a threat to the economies of the world and an arms race squanders vast resources that are desperately needed to ameliorate economic and social privations that give rise to national unrest. As we have indicated, without enhanced social justice one cannot expect passive acceptance of the prescribed order. Peace is essential, but there can be no peace without justice and no justice without peace.

If one recalls that the present international community consists of nearly 160 sovereign nations, it will be apparent that obtaining universal, or near-universal, concurrence to a major revision of the prevailing order is not something that can be easily achieved. As prevailing educational and economic inequalities are diminished, and as ideological rivalries gradually become less strident and intolerant than they are today, the pace of progress may be enhanced — but it will take time. As long as the required elements of law, courts and enforcement (including its related components: improved international agencies, disarmament, sanctions and social justice) are lacking, powerful international adversaries will see no choice but to arm themselves and prepare for the defense of their perceived vital interests. Like an intricate jigsaw puzzle, all of the pieces must fit together and be in place before the picture of a more tranquil world can emerge as an acceptable alternative to the present system of terror.

This study has been divided into three parts. Part One seeks to set forth the historical evolutionary trends to demonstrate how far we have come in developing each of the components required for a peaceful world. The reader interested in history should be able to confirm that the development of international law was a slow and erratic process that was based on many centuries of thought and that only during the past 200 years has it begun to flower. International courts only began to be accepted after the first World War. The process of enforcing international law — together with its supporting elements — was only seriously acted upon during the last few decades. All of these developments must mature and become functional before anything resembling international peace can be anticipated. The fact that progress is being made should encourage those who might otherwise despair. The Second Part outlines what needs to be done — what *should* be done to strengthen the components that must be in place before peace can become a reality. These suggestions are not inflexible nor definitive mandates. They appeal to the reader's common sense and should enable him or her to focus on the essence of what is required. The Third Part — examining what really *can* be done — is the most difficult. We must deal with the world and its problems as we find it. But there are many constructive steps that should and can be taken to help ameliorate contemporary conflicts and to build a more peaceful world in the future.

It is my hope that readers will gain sufficient knowledge and confidence that they will not succumb to the temptation to leave these difficult matters to the so-called experts. Sovereign states, both large and small, should come to realize that it is in their own self-interest to support all those measures that point toward a society in which the role of international law, courts and enforcement is strengthened. All actions or proposals by governments or bureaucrats that move in an opposite direction should be resisted. Rational human beings everywhere — regardless of nationality, political or religious persuasion — long for peace. If Decision-Makers do not see clearly in which direction nations should be moving, they will never lead the people to their desired goal. If leaders are unable to satisfy the common aspirations of humankind, it will be up to the people themselves — better informed, better educated, better organized and more united — to assert their democratic and human right to live in peace and dignity. In this interdependent world, the sovereignty of the state must yield to the sovereignty of the law. If the common sense reasoning I have expounded seems to be Utopian, let the reader ponder the alternatives.

There are those who may argue that the effort to construct a global consensus capable of constraining the aggressive behavior of states is a futile enterprise. They will point out, no doubt correctly, that ever since the time of Thucydides, national leaders have always done what they believed — rightly or wrongly — to be in their own best interests. Only in rare instances, when strength was nicely balanced, did sovereigns recognize that war was a hazardous enterprise and they therefore refrained from the use of force. The argument fails adequately to take into account that, if fear served to deter wars in the past, it should serve as an even greater deterrent in the nuclear age. The non-use of force is now a matter of *EVERYONE'S* self-interest.

I am grateful to many distinguished scholars and statesmen who have, in their writings, recognized that reason must triumph over rage if we are to survive. I have tried to reinforce their arguments by adding the historical proof that progress is in fact being made. Demonstrating that everything is linked may help to explain some of the difficulties and encourage a broader sweep of effort. Bureaucratic tyranny can never be allowed to be the last word. I have noted in conclusion that there is no reason to despair. Whether we choose to walk toward the high ground or over the precipice depends on us.

Teachers — particularly of peace studies, political science or public international law — may find in the present focus on law, courts and enforcement a common-sense concept within which to embrace the facts that must be mastered for a comprehensive and realistic appraisal of the obstacles to be overcome. It is hoped that this small volume will lend some measure of encouragement as well as enlightenment to all those concerned with resolving the difficult and urgent problems of world peace. I wish to express my appreciation to Professor Myres M. McDougal of Yale whose writings on behalf of human rights have been an inspiration and for his comments regarding an outline of this book. Steve Wasserman, Editor of New Republic Books, made a number of perceptive observations that have helped to sharpen my thinking on critical issues. My wife, Gertrude, has — as always — been consistently helpful and encouraging. And special thanks to my publisher, Philip F. Cohen.

BENJAMIN B. FERENCZ
Adjunct Professor
Pace University School of Law
Teaching "The International Law of Peace"

New York, August, 1985

"In the following pages I offer nothing more than simple facts, plain arguments, and common sense; and have no other preliminaries to settle with the reader, than that he will divest himself of prejudice and prepossession, and suffer his reason and his feelings to determine for themselves. . ."

From *Common Sense,* by Thomas Paine, 1776.

PART ONE: WHAT *HAS* BEEN DONE

I. *The Growth of International Law*

Without laws or accepted standards specifying the permissible limits of international behavior, there can be no peaceful world. Primitive law led to national law which, in turn, led to international law. How far have we come and where do we stand in this evolutionary process?

A. INTERNATIONAL LAW TAKES ROOT

A review of the historical record reveals that as long as man can remember, he has been governed by rules prescribing what he may and may not do. Long before the Christian era, renowned tables of the law —attributed to Divine origin or inspiration — were developed by such persons as Menes (who governed Egypt three thousand years before the birth of Christ,) Hammurabi (who ruled Babylonia a thousand years later,) Moses (who lived in the thirteenth century B.C.,) Draco and Solon (who influenced Greece in the seventh century B.C.,) and, a few centuries later, Mencius and Confucius in China and Manu in India. From these primitive origins would come national and, eventually, international law.

Rules for waging war laid the foundation for international law. The ancient Romans were among the first to formulate elaborate regulations to govern the use of force against a foreign adversary. Roman law decreed that before war could be declared, the enemy had to be informed of the complaint and be given a set time in which to comply. Only the Roman Senate could authorize armed conflict. As Cicero (106-43 B.C.) pointed out, wars had to be legally declared, waged only for a just cause (such as in defense of territory, to protect honor or safety, or to enforce a solemn obligation) and honorably fought. The declaration of war had to be accompanied by special incantations or rituals, such as hurling a javelin upon the land of the enemy. Those who waged war illegally by violating the rules would be handed over to the enemy in order that punishment would fall only upon the offender and not on the innocent public. Roman law and justice helped to maintain peace throughout the vast Roman imperium for two hundred years.

Another highlight in the development of law took place on the fields of Runnymede where, in 1216, the nobles of England forced King John to sign the *Magna Carta,* promising to uphold feudal customs and the rights of the aristocracy. With the decline of feudalism, mercantilism became the life-blood of European states and laws that had initially governed relatively small homogenous groups dwelling in limited geographical areas had to be expanded to meet the needs of a changing society. In what may be seen as the beginnings of international criminal law, pirates — who threatened the free flow of commerce — were outlawed as "the enemies of all mankind" who could be tried and punished wherever they might be seized. Maritime Consuls and Guilds gradually developed specific rules for the orderly regulation of international commerce.

With the discovery of America, the monarchs of Europe saw the fresh terrain as a new source of glory, dominion and riches. The medieval theology of the crusades had taught that subjugating infidels was carrying out God's will and that non-Christians were barbarians, undeserving of human consideration. But the genocidal slaughter of the Incas of South America by Spanish Conquistadores sparked theological reexamination of the duties of states in the application of God's universal laws. One profound lover of mankind who dared to question the prevailing practices was Franciscus de Victoria, a Spaniard who had studied at the Sorbonne in Paris before being named Primary Professor of Sacred Theology at the University of Salamanca in 1526. Influenced by the writings of Cicero, the Reverend Father taught that all wars had to be morally justifiable — to right a wrong. Even in self-defense, he said, one was bound to do as little harm as possible to the enemy. According to Victoria, differences of religion or the personal glory of a prince were not acceptable reasons for waging war; no subject was bound to serve in an unjust war, even if commanded by his sovereign. The learned Jesuit was far ahead of his time. Victoria's lectures, assembled from notes taken by his students, could only be published 150 years after his death. Today, Victoria is recognized and acclaimed as one of the founders of international law.

The man usually hailed as the father of international law is the great Dutch jurist, Huig von Groot, more commonly known as Hugo Grotius. He enjoyed a successful legal career, wrote extensively, and was active in local politics. When an opposition party seized power, Grotius was sentenced to life imprisonment. Although in confinement, he had access to classical writings and he composed his thoughts on the nature of jurisprudence and relations among states. He managed to escape, and, in 1625, completed his famous treatise *Three Books on the Laws of War and Peace.* It was a poetical and philosophical study that drew upon the learned writers of the past. His review of history led him to espouse the brotherhood of man and the need to treat all people fairly. He argued that the only way for weak nations to prevail against more powerful ones was for them to unite in creating laws and institutions that could enforce justice. According to Grotius, the lack of binding legal precedents to settle disputes among states made war unavoidable; the absence of an effective court made war inevitable. Wars, he said, could legitimately be waged only against "those who were the first to inflict injury." Justice and honor were obligatory under all circumstances and those who wrongfully caused a war would be answerable for their wrongdoing. True repentence required restitution. He appealed for humane conduct even in warfare, "Lest by imitating wild beasts too much we forget to be human." Grotius listed three methods to prevent violence between nations: 1- conferences, 2- arbitration, or 3- by lot — as had been suggested by Solomon. As a much lesser evil than war between armies, he mentioned that heads of state might settle their differences by single combat between themselves — an idea that may appear particularly tempting in the nuclear age.

The present system of independent nation states is usually traced back to the Treaties of Westphalia in 1648. Heidelberg was the first university to establish a chair in international law and its first professor of international law was Samuel Pufendorf, who published *On the Law of Nature and Nations,* in 1688. It was almost a century later before the American continent could produce any significant landmark in the development of law. In 1777, thirteen British colonies declared themselves to be free and independent states. When they adopted Articles of Confederation and Perpetual Union, a Constitution of the United States of America and a Bill of Rights, it was an inspiring leap forward in international law. These legal documents showed how sovereign states — that had formerly been colonies of the Crown — could, by common consent, join in a new and united confederation with an elected legislature that could enact laws that would bind the entire community. A Supreme Court and an Executive would maintain peace and justice among the states and assure that the rights of all citizens were protected. Even the phrase "international law" was practically unknown until it gained prominence for the first time when Jeremy Bentham, around 1793, published *Principles of International Law.* One should be reminded that these developments took place only during the past few centuries.

The ideas of Cicero, Grotius and others calling for humane behavior even among adversaries began to be codified in the midst of the American civil war. President Abraham Lincoln called upon Francis Lieber, a former Prussian officer who had become a teacher at Columbia college in New York, to draft a code that might help to alleviate some of the anguish of the sick, wounded and prisoners-of-war. The Lieber Code was enacted in 1863 and became the model for similar codes later adopted by the International Committee of the Red Cross and accepted and expanded by many nations. Lieber's friend, Professor Johann Caspar Bluntschli of Heidelberg, soon drafted another code which, in 862 articles, sought to define the laws of war and peace. In 1872, David Dudley Field, who had codified the laws of the state of New York and was the first President of the unofficial International Law Association, drafted *Outlines of an International Code,* which called for arbitration of disputes and collective enforcement action. Similar codes of international law were proposed by other distinguished authorities in other parts of the world. Among the most notable were those by Professor James Lorimer of Edinburgh, in 1884, and Professor Pasquale Fiore of Italy, in 1890, who — for the first time — referred to "the scourge of war" as the "greatest of all crimes." The seeds of international law were slowly taking root.

B. THE GROWTH OF LAW FROM 1899 TO 1945

It took thousands of years to move from the primitive law of the pre-Christian era to the beginnings of what might be considered international law. Although, during the past few centuries, the seeds of international law were beginning to take root, in matters conceived to be of vital importance, sovereign states continued to look to their guns rather than to the emerging law of nations. Reliance on arms rather than law was — then as now — a very costly matter. In an attempt to relieve the very heavy burden of an arms race, the Czar of Russia, in 1899, proposed that twenty-six (self-styled) "civilized states" convene at the Hague for what was heralded as the first "International Peace Conference."

When the second Hague Conference was convened, in 1907, the number of participants was increased to forty-four — which was a form of progress —and the 1899 Conventions were revised. A number of new Conventions were added at this "Second International Peace Conference" but twelve out of fourteen related to rules for military combat. There was no fundamental change in the attitude of states. The tradition of sovereignty was so firmly entrenched that nations did not see the necessity for accepting more meaningful limitations on their ability to pursue their goals by the use of armed might.

The limited progress that was made at the Hague could not prevent the outbreak of the first World War. From 1914 to 1918, nations were so busy trying to destroy each other that there was neither time nor inclination for further codification of international law. When the agony was over, Decision-Makers began to re-think their past positions that had led them to such a sorry state. French Foreign Minister and Nobel-Prize winner Léon Bourgeois, who had played a key role at the Hague conferences, looked back and explained:

> We did not see clearly enough that in the society of states, just as in relations of individuals, there is no lasting peace without judicial organization... The definition of the rights of nations and the organization of a jurisdiction destined to guarantee them are thus the essential conditions for the establishment and maintenance of peace.

The next significant milestone in man's attempt to clarify the norms of international behavior was reached after World War I with the signing of the Covenant of the League of Nations in 1919. The High

Contracting Parties (consisting of fifty-three nations) confirmed their common plan to achieve international peace and security:

> by the acceptance of obligations not to resort to war, by the prescription of open, just and honorable relations between nations, by the firm establishment of the understandings of internationl law as the actual rule of conduct among Governments, and by the maintenance of justice and a scrupulous respect for all treaty obligations in the dealings of organized peoples with one another.

For the first time, a large number of powerful nations were able to recognize and confirm the importance of law as a vital component of international peace.

In 1924, the League appointed a Committee of Experts for the Progressive Codification of International Law. The use of the term "progressive" was an acknowledgment that law was not static but had to be adapted to meet the needs of a society that was in constant flux. The Committee consisted of seventeen experts representing "the main forms of civilization and the principal legal systems of the world" — thus recognizing that codification of law should be a democratic process which would seek to reconcile diverse views which were entitled to be heard. In his message to the Congress that year, President Calvin Coolidge expressed his specific support for codification of international law, and Elihu Root, who had been the U.S. Secretary of State and American representative at the Hague (he was also the founder and President of the American Society of International Law) saw in codification the natural evolution of international law. Other American scholars echoed the same sentiment.

While the Codification Committee was at work, the League reiterated the obligation of all members to settle their disputes by peaceful means and declared that all wars of aggression "shall always be prohibited." This led to the widely-acclaimed Kellogg-Briand Pact of 1928 which renounced war as an instrument of national policy. But, in an exchange of letters, the major powers reserved to themselves the "inherent right" to decide when they would be acting in lawful "self-defense". Obviously, the distinction between "aggression" and "self-defense" required legal clarification and a special group of experts was assigned to deal with that specific problem.

The experts dealing with the definition of aggression had no doubt that sending a hostile army across the frontier of a friendly neighboring state was an illegal act. But they were by no means agreed regarding indirect acts of subversion, or threats, or a disproportionate response to a relatively minor provocation. It soon became clear, as it did in the Codification Committee, that powerful states were not really willing to tie their own hands. It was concluded, therefore, that no general definition of aggression was feasible, or desirable, and that each case of alleged agression would have to be considered on its own special facts and circumstances. The unwillingness of leading nations to define the conditions under which they could lawfully resort to arms would make it impossible to maintain peace.

The highlights on the road toward the codification of international law reveal that the Hague Conferences of 1899 and 1907 made their most significant contribution in clarifying certain rules of war. The 1919 Covenant of the League was the first widely-accepted declaration of general principles of desirable international behavior and was a major step forward. The first committee specifically charged with the general codification of international law required five years before it could even outline the subjects considered amenable to legal particularization. The definition of acts that would constitute unlawful aggression was not something upon which agreement could be reached. By 1937, it was clear that nations were not ready to bind themselves either to define aggression, prohibit terrorism or create an international court to deal with such offenses. Unwilling to honor the principles they were pledged to accept, and unprepared to take measures to curb international terrorism, nations would — by 1939 — find themselves the victims of aggression and state terrorism on a scale never before experienced in human history. It would take another world war to stimulate nations to take additional steps to clarify and codify the norms of international behavior.

C. THE BURST OF CODIFICATION AFTER 1945

The 1945 Charter of the United Nations may properly be regarded as one of the great acts of codification of international law. All members of the organization agreed to be legally bound by the obligations spelled out in the founding instrument. Chapter I declared the purposes of the organization: to maintain international peace and security, to take effective collective measures to remove threats to the peace, to suppress acts of aggression or other breaches of the peace and to settle disputes by peaceful means "in conformity with the principles of justice and international law." It referred to developing friendly relations among nations based on equal rights and self-determination, and of international cooperation in promoting human rights and fundamental freedoms. Members were enjoined from the threat or use of force except in accordance with the terms of the Charter. Although subsequent elaboration of rules to spell out these obligations in greater detail would be required, these general principles constituted a legal framework binding upon all.

Those who drafted the Charter were not prepared to invest the United Nations with legislative authority to enact binding international laws. To minimize the impact of that shortcoming, and to continue the codification work that had been started by the League, the Charter obligated the General Assembly to encourage "the progressive development of international law and its codification." In January, 1947, the Assembly established a committee to deal with that task and later the assignment was taken over by an International Law Commission (ILC) that was answerable to the Assembly.

Over the years, the ILC has painstakingly formulated many legal principles which were considered to be deserving of general acceptance as binding international law. In 1949, the Commission submitted a Draft Declaration on the Rights and Duties of States. It was intended to proclaim "the supremacy of international law" and to serve as a foundation for the formulation of more precise rules that would give effect to the general statement of basic rights and duties of all nations. The following year, the ILC formulated principles of international law that had been recognized in the Charter and Judgment of the International Military Tribunal that had tried German war criminals at Nuremberg. Under the stimulus of those prosecutions, the General Assembly approved a Genocide Convention intended to prevent the recurrence of that crime. The ILC was asked to consider problems related to the creation of a permanent International Criminal Court for the trial of persons who might be accused of crimes against humanity. Soon, the question of international criminal jurisdiction became intertwined with the problem of defining aggression and of drafting a code of offenses against the peace and security of mankind. Progress in these sensitive areas was impeded after 1954 by rivalries and antagonisms between the major powers, but the work done in the Commission served to clarify, if not resolve, the differences and difficulties that had to be overcome.

In addition to codification by specific multinational conventions, customary international law is being further clarified and confirmed by the regular publication of information showing the development and acceptance of laws by different sovereign states. All international courts publish annual reports of their decisions. Treaties signed between nations become a source of international law. Professor Louis Sohn has pointed out that more treaties have been concluded since 1945 than in the preceeding two thousand years; each one limits the sovereignty of the signatories to some extent.

The General Assembly itself has frequently taken the initiative through its Resolutions and Declarations to clarify what the law is or ought to be. It has appointed Special Committees to deal with particularly difficult problems and these Committees provide still another forum in which the legal obligations of states are clarified and defined. One of the best known and widely accepted attempts at clarification of international norms was the Universal Declaration of Human Rights, adopted by the General Assembly in 1948. This Declaration articulated the common aspiration of all people for freedom, justice and peace in a spirit of universal brotherhood. It recognized the inherent dignity of all members of the human family. Many specific rights — such as the right to life, liberty and security — were enumerated. The Universal Declaration was later supplemented by Covenants setting forth more precise civil and political, a well as economic, social and cultural rights for all peoples. Even though these legal instruments did not constitute binding international law, they set standards to which the signatories aspired and they encouraged the enactment of national laws to enforce the human rights objectives. In 1960, the Assembly, reaffirming "faith in fundamental human rights, in the dignity and worth of the human person, in the equal rights of men and women and of nations large and small," adopted a Declaration on the Granting of Independence to Colonial Countries and Peoples. It proclaimed that subjecting peoples to alien domination and exploitation was a denial of fundamental rights and an impediment to world peace. The Declaration encouraged the emancipation of scores of colonies, allowing them to take their rightful place as independent partners of the world community.

Other notable instruments adopted by consensus during the ensuing years include the 1970 Declaration on Principles of International Law Concerning Friendly Relations and Cooperation Among States. It clarified such precepts as the non-use of force, the need for peaceful settlement of disputes, non-intervention in the internal affairs of other states, and the equal rights of all peoples. Conventions were signed by many nations agreeing to suppress unlawful seizures of aircraft and to treat aerial hijackers as pirates. Ninety states voted to punish apartheid —irrespective of motive. Conventions were adopted that outlawed certain crimes against diplomats. The definition of aggression — adopted by consensus after some fifty years of effort —condemned acts of covert subversion as well as overt attacks and (despite many shortcomings) opened the door to further work on the draft code of offenses against the peace and security of mankind that had been left pending. All of these legal instruments were clear evidence of the unremitting desire of most members of the international community to replace the law of force by the force of law.

In 1975, thirty-five nations — including the United States and the Soviet Union — signed the Helsinki Final Act of the Conference on Security and Cooperation in Europe. Putting aside their fundamental political and socio-economic rivalries, the nations concerned agreed to support a wide array of human rights objectives. Cooperation was promised in economics, science, technology and increased educational and cultural exchanges. "Confidence-building measures" were to be enhanced. It was agreed that there would be public follow-up conferences to monitor compliance by the signatories. In 1979, a Convention against the Taking of Hostages was adopted by one hundred and eighteen nations that agreed to curb terrorism and its causes. The Economic Rights and Duties of States became a renewed topic of debate. A consensus was reached in Manila, in 1982, concerning a Declaration on the Peaceful Settlement of International Disputes; it specificaly recognized the importance of codification of international law. Later that year, after more than fourteen years of intensive effort, the Final Act was signed for a monumental Law of the Sea. The burst of codification efforts that accelerated during the 1970's was unparalleled. It was as though even skeptical diplomats were beginning to sense that without broad acceptance of new standards, the hopes of peoples would not be fulfilled and the world could not long survive.

The international instruments that were — in ever increasing numbers — accepted by consensus or overwhelming vote to clarify the rules of international behavior were, like most innovations, far from perfect. Some nations and groups insisted that their own goals were so legitimate and their own power so limited that it was necessary, and legally permissible, to use every available means to attain their particular ends. Others felt that codification was not really necessary since their own domestic legislation already prohibited impermissible behavior. In order to reach consensus, key provisions were often left deliberately vague and amenable to conflicting interpretations. Imperfect as they were, the significance of these measures lay in the fact that even moral obligations — if widely heralded and acclaimed — have a way of growing into accepted canons of binding international law, and of attracting sufficient support to make flouting them a perilous adventure. The very process of negotiating a complicated accord among many nations with sharply differing legal standards, traditions and ideologies was in itself an important advance. Techniques for drafting complicated legal instruments were developed and states were learning to understand each other better and to overcome differences by talking rather than fighting. Policy-Makers were seeing just how complex it is to reconcile and synthesize diverse goals and values, and that codification of law, though vital, is only one part of a more complicated and continuing evolutionary process leading toward compliance with common standards in a peaceful world.

II. *Utilizing International Tribunals*

Just as the growth of law from earliest times was a slow and difficult — but continually accelerating process — history reveals a similar evolutionary pattern regarding the use of judicial-type proceedings to settle international disputes by peaceful means.

A. ORIGINS AND BEGINNINGS

We have noted that when the British colonies in America declared their independence they agreed to be bound by the judgment of a Supreme Court with authority to interpret the Constitution and to adjudicate whatever controversies might arise between the states of the new Union. This concept of an independent tribunal with exclusive and compulsory jurisdiction to resolve conflicts between sovereign states that have joined together in a new federation was a vital part of the structure of the United States of America when the nation was formed. The idea of turning to peaceful settlement rather than to the battlefield was reinforced when the fledgling nation agreed, in the Jay Treaty of 1794, to resolve border disputes with the former mother country by binding decisions of mixed arbitral commissions. The early agreements to rely on judicial-type proceedings helped to maintain peace between the United States and Great Britain ever since the American revolution.

The first effort to establish a permanent court of arbitration took place during the Hague Conferences of 1899. The Convention for the Pacific Settlement of International Disputes contained a recommendation for mediation, provisions for commissions of inquiry and what appeared to be a system for peaceful settlement by a Permanent Court of Arbitration (PCA). A number of qualifying clauses showed, however, that the participants were not ready to commit themselves unconditionally to abandonment of force. The signatories agreed only to "use their best efforts" and to avoid recourse to arms "as far as possible," and to turn to mediation "as far as circumstances allow." Even where good offices of third parties were requested by those involved in a dispute, the recommendations would "have exclusively the character of advice and never have binding force."

The statutes of the Permanent Court of Arbitration reflected the hesitancy of sovereign states to restrict their own freedom of action. The title of the PCA was largely a misnomer; it was not permanent and it was not a court. It was a list of some 150 to 200 persons who agreed to be available when and if the parties to a dispute might call upon them for assistance. The only thing permanent about the PCA was its location; it was established in the Hague and is still there today. In almost eighty years, it has decided about two dozen cases, none of which concerned vital interests. Despite the hesitation of states to accept an effective arbitral tribunal with broad authority, the principle of obligatory arbitration was widely endorsed, and many nations entered into bilateral treaties providing for the general arbitration of disputes.

During the course of the Second Hague Conference, Great Britain had nearly been drawn into Russia's war with Japan when Russia had fired upon a British ship in the North Sea. Britain was eager to clarify the rights of warring states to seize foreign ships as prizes of war. Most sea-faring nations had their own courts to rule on the validity of such captures, but the national tribunals were seen as self-serving and their decisions often provoked reprisals or conflict. Several international law associations had recommended that appeals from national prize courts should be heard by an International Prize Tribunal. Great Britain took the lead in preparing a draft convention for such a court, to be composed of fifteen judges representing different legal systems. It would apply "rules of international law" as well as "general principles of justice and equity." The court was to sit in the Hague and use the available facilities of the PCA. What made this particular convention so unique and important was that all of the signatories would become subject to the compulsory jurisdiction of the Tribunal. When the convention was promptly signed by thirty-nine states, it was seen as a great step forward in the development of international law. The proposed Tribunal was hailed as "the first truly organized international court in the history of the world." His Majesty's Government called it "an inestimable service to civilization and mankind." The American delegate, James Brown Scott, wrote: "The hope of the dreamer has been realized." He saw the Prize Court as a precedent for "the establishment of an international tribunal for the trial and settlement of international controversies arising in time of peace." In addressing Congress in 1907, President Theodore Roosevelt referred to "the great advance which the world is making toward the substitution of the rule of reason and justice in place of simple force."

The signing of the Convention was, however, only the first step; ratifications were necessary. Once the war-time hazard that had stimulated the desire for international controls had disappeared, it began to appear that the high praise for the Prize Court had been premature. Several Powers began to express some apprehension about the uncertainty or imprecision of such vague standards as the "rules of international law" and the "principles of justice and equity" which the new Prize Court was expected to apply. Britain invited ten leading maritime nations to meet in order to try to specify the exact terms of the laws which would govern the proposed new court. The London Naval Conference of 1908-1909 drew up a code which dealt with such subjects as the rules for blockade and the permissible bounds of search and seizure of vessels in time of war. The Declaration that emerged from the conference was signed by all of the participants — but the House of Lords, fearing that British food might be intercepted, refused to ratify the rules. The acceptance of the Prize Court had been made conditional upon Britain's acceptance of the Code of Naval Law; when the Code was rejected, the Court was doomed.

At the other side of the globe, a Central American Court of Justice came into existence in 1908 pursuant to a convention that was part of a peace treaty signed by several Central American Republics that had been at war with each other. The Court was composed of five judges elected by the national legislatures of the five participating states. The Court's decisions were to be final and each signatory agreed to be bound by the Court's judgments. The Convention was scheduled to expire in ten years. During the period 1908-1918, ten cases came before the tribunal. It rendered an affirmative judgment in only two cases but an interlocutory decree — in a complaint by Honduras that Guatemala and El Salvador were supporting a revolution against Honduras — may have prevented a new Central American war. Unfortunately, the mandate of the Court was never renewed; nations were too concerned with the world war to pay much attention to the modalities for maintaining peace. Despite its limited accomplishments and duration, it should be borne in mind that the Central American Court of Justice was the first permanent international tribunal in the history of man.

Both the aborted International Prize Court and the Central American Court reflected the hopes that the judicial process would become a substitute for the use of force. Many statesmen had recognized that binding arbitration or an international court would be a better method for settling international disputes than war. When Theodore Roosevelt was awarded the Nobel Peace-Prize in 1910, he noted in his acceptance speech that a League of Peace, formed by the Great Powers, could prevent the peace from being broken. "All mankind," he said, "would be grateful for all time to the statesman who could bring about a new structure of international society." Later that same year, President Howard Taft, addressing the American Society for the Judicial Settlement of International Disputes, declared:

> I am strongly convinced that the best method of ultimately securing disarmament is the establishment of an international court and the development of a code of international equity which nations will recognize as affording a better method of settling international controversies than war.

The American Society of International Law also gave its full support to the objective of establishing a permanent international tribunal. Leading peace societies urged the United States to sign an arbitration treaty with Great Britain that would cover all disputes between them — without any reservations. An international association of legal scholars, meeting in 1912, called for unrestricted compulsory arbitration of all disputes between states.

While Decision-Makers were vacillating, they were overtaken by events that might have been anticipated. Europe was a powder-keg waiting to explode; the assassination of the Austrian Archduke at Sarajevo in June, 1914 was the spark. No international system for binding arbitration or the judicial settlement of disputes had been created. There was a heavy price to pay for the indecision. In the absence of any court or similar organization competent to compel a peaceful settlement, the parties were left with only one alternative — to call upon their military alliances and to try to settle the issues by force of arms. Humankind was engulfed in its first World War — which, as history would show, settled nothing.

B. LIMITED ACCEPTANCE

Hopes for a better world after World War I were to rest on the twin pillars of a League of Nations and the rule of law. As part of the Preliminary Peace Conference, a 15-member Commission was appointed to consider "The Responsibility of the Author's of the War." Its presiding officer was U.S. Secretary of State Robert Lansing, assisted by Major James Brown Scott, Judge Advocate of the U.S. Army, who had been at the Hague Conferences and who was a strong advocate of an international court. In addition to condemning aggressive war, the Commission set out facts which showed that the Hague agreements on the rules of war had been deliberately breached by such atrocities as the killing of hostages, the use of poison gas, the massacre of civilians, attacks on hospital ships, and a long list of similar crimes "to the eternal shame of those who committed them." For the first time, consideration was given to the establishment of an international court to deal with the crimes of war.

The Commission proposed that a High Tribunal should be created. It would be composed of twenty-two judges from the allied nations. The international court would have authority to try even a head of state. The Commission felt that to grant immunity to a sovereign:

> would involve laying down the principle that the greatest outrages against the laws and customs of war and the laws of humanity, if proved against him, could in no circumstances be punished. Such a conclusion would shock the conscience of civilized mankind.

But, in the light of doubts expressed by Secretary Lansing and the Japanese member, the Commission finally concluded that international law had not yet advanced to a stage where a premeditated war of aggression could be treated as a punishable crime. To correct this shortcoming, the Commission recommended that "for the future penal sanctions should be provided for such grave outrages against the elementary principles of international law."

The Treaty of Versailles did not mention the crime of aggression; instead, it provided in Article 227 that the Kaiser would have to stand trial for "a supreme offense against international morality and the sanctity of treaties." He was to be tried by a special tribunal of five judges appointed by the major victorious powers. Articles 228 and 229 required Germany to hand over for trial by allied military tribunals all those who had committed crimes in violation of the laws and customs of war. Although Germany signed the treaty, it was quickly denounced as a *Diktat* and Germany refused to hand over any of its soldiers for trial by a court of former enemies. The Kaiser found asylum in neutral Holland which refused to extradite him. In the end, the Kaiser escaped trial completely and the Allies agreed that Germany could try its own war criminals — which turned out to be rather a farce. The first effort to introduce a rule of international criminal law for the punishment of aggressors and war criminals had gotten off to a slow start — but it would serve as a stepping stone for later legal advances.

The Covenant of the League of Nations called for the establishment of a Permanent Court of International Justice (PCIJ). It was to be vested with authority to render advisory opinions on any dispute or question submitted to it by the Council or the Assembly of the League. But the Court would only have jurisdiction to hear and determine such disputes of an international character "which the parties thereto shall submit to it." In February, 1920, ten experts — chosen from among the most eminent legal authorities — were designated as an Advisory Committee of Jurists and authorized to draw up plans for the creation of the court described in the Covenant. Even though the United States was not a member of the League (and never would become one,) the Advisory Committee included Elihu Root and his assistant James Brown Scott among the distinguished experts. The Jurists did not fail to notice that their mandate called for them to draw up statutes for a court that would have no compulsory jurisdiction and therefore could have only very limited power. They sought to overcome those restraints, however, by an interpretation which would have given the Court greater competence and authority. The full Legal Committee of the League —to which the Jurists had to report — did not choose to consider the advantages which would result from a system of compulsory jurisdiction. Instead, they felt that the Jurists' interpretation — that accepting the Statute would automatically amount to submission to the Court — had gone too far and was inconsistent with the Covenant. The Jurists' recommendations were rejected.

A number of nations spoke out in favor of an international court with compulsory jurisdiction. A prophetic Italian delegate warned that if states were allowed to resort to war instead of being required to appear before a court, "The Tribunal will disappear and with it the League of Nations." But they could not prevail against the powerful opposition of Great Britain. Conservative leader Mr. Balfour made the British position quite clear: "We desire to see the applications to that Court made voluntarily and not compulsorily." Judge Loder of the Supreme Court of the Netherlands bitterly denounced the British argument that "the time is not yet ripe" as a political ploy to which the Committee had been forced to yield. "Well," said Judge Loder, "we will go more slowly if you desire, even to the point of almost losing an opportunity of going forward. You desire that today shall be yours; today therefore shall be yours; but tomorrow will be ours." The most that could be achieved was the acceptance of a Swiss compromise proposal (Article 36) which offered states an option whether or not and to what extent to accept the Court's jurisdiction. The expert Jurists did their best to establish a stronger judicial structure but their efforts were defeated by others who chose to look to the past rather than to the future.

The Committee of Jurists tried — again unsuccessfully — to exceed their mandate in another very important respect. Mr. Root drew attention to the fact that the proper organization of international justice also required consideration of a High Court of International Justice "to try crimes against international public order and the universal law of nations." Several members agreed that it would be wise to try to set up such a tribunal rather than run the risk of being accused of creating one *ex post facto* after a war. But the majority was unwilling to go beyond the limited parameters prescribed by the Covenant.

By 1922, the Permanent Court of International Justice was inaugurated. Fourteen states accepted the "optional clause" in Article 36 of the Statute, thus agreeing to submit at least some disputes to judicial adjudication. This significant number of acceptances was seen as a very favorable sign — even though several major powers were conspicuous by their reticence. Judge Loder wrote:

There does not seem to be any doubt that the future will

bring compulsory jurisdiction between states. . . Great
nations will see that bluster and threats will be of no avail,
and that they are impeded by rigid confinement within their
own conception of sovereignty. It will be realized that all of
this belongs to an obsolete world order.

The isolationists in the U.S. Senate, who had successfully blocked
America's becoming a member of the League, eventually consented to
U.S. adherence to the PCIJ — but only subject to reservations which
made it clear that the Court could only act on American issues when,
and if, it suited the United States.

Despite its serious deficiencies, the PCIJ was an improvement upon
what had existed before that time. In contrast with the so-called
Permanent Court of Arbitration that had been established in the Hague
in 1899, the PCIJ was not merely a list of available arbitrators who
might be called upon when needed but was a permanent institution with
a permanent location, secretariat and independent judges appointed for
nine-year terms. The problem of selecting suitable judges — which had
proved to be an insurmountable barrier in the Hague in 1907, had been
resolved.

During the relatively brief period of its activity — from 1922 to 1939
when it was interrupted by war — the PCIJ rendered twenty-six
advisory opinions, issued judgments in twenty-two cases and was named
an intermediary to resolve conflicting interpretations in hundreds of
international agreements. Its decisions made a significant contribution
to the clarification and development of international law and the
interpretation of treaties. The gradual improvement of international
judicial procedures was another significant achievement. The experience
of the PCIJ served as the foundation stone for its successor, the
International Court of Justice that was to be established after World
War II.

C. EXPANSION OF THE JUDICIAL PROCESS

The utilization of the judicial process after World War II expanded
in several directions: International Military Tribunals were created to
punish war criminals, the World Court was improved, many regional
courts came into existence and administrative tribunals of all kinds
began to flourish.

One of the most urgent political problems after the second world
war — just as it had been after World War I — was to bring to speedy
justice those who had initiated the wars of aggression or had been
responsible for committing atrocities on a scale never before seen in
human history. The German leaders had repeatedly been warned that
they would be held to account for their crimes. Both Great Britain and
the United States were determined that the failures regarding the trial of
war criminals after World War I would not be repeated. The proposals
for an International Criminal Court that had been allowed to lie
dormant after the first World War served as the basis for renewed

deliberations. By 1943, the London International Assembly, an unofficial group of legal experts who had been forced to flee from countries overrun by Germany, drafted a comprehensive Convention for the Creation of an International Criminal Court. Professor Lauterpacht of Cambridge wrote: "There appear to be compelling reasons for the establishment in the future of an International Criminal Court having jurisdiction to try the crimes of war (i.e. resort to war in violation of international law.)" Professor Hans Kelsen wrote that only international jurisdiction could cope with war crimes, and treaties establishing an International Court with compulsory jurisdiction was "the first and indispensable step to an effective reform of international relations."

By the beginning of 1945, with German defeat imminent, the United States took the lead in setting up an international tribunal for the trial of major German war criminals. Robert H. Jackson, on leave from the U.S. Supreme Court, had been assigned by the President to make the necessary arrangements. Jackson warned that sterile legalisms should not be allowed to defeat the common sense of justice. "It is high time," he said, "that we act on the juridical principle that aggressive war-making is illegal and criminal."

In June, 1945, a negotiating conference took place in London for the purpose of coordinating the views of the four Allied governments that had occupied Germany — the U.S., U.K., U.S.S.R., and France. In less than six weeks, a compromise text was agreed upon and on August 8th, 1945, the Charter for the first International Military Tribunal in history was signed. It called for "just and prompt trial and punishment of the major war criminals of the European Axis." The Tribunal was to consist of one representative from each of the four Powers; conviction would require the vote of three. The Court was to have jurisdiction over three categories of crime: Crimes against Peace — which meant the preparation or waging of a war of aggression; War Crimes — namely, violating the laws and customs of war, and Crimes against Humanity —such as extermination, enslavement and other inhumane acts committed against a civilian population. The IMT Charter and its rules of procedure to guarantee a fair trial represented the culmination of thinking and preparatory work that had taken place many years before. As a consequence, the world's first international penal court was soon ready for its first case.

Twenty-four major Nazi war criminals were indicted in the Court house at Nuremberg on October 18, 1945 and accused of a conspiracy to commit Crimes against Peace, War Crimes and Crimes against Humanity; the particulars were spelled out in abundant detail. The opening statement by United States Chief Prosecutor Jackson gave assurance that the fundamental purpose of the prosecution was the advancement of law and justice:

> The common sense of mankind demands that law shall not
> stop with the punishment of petty crimes by little people . . .
> We must never forget that the record on which we judge

these defendants today is the record on which history will judge us tomorrow. To pass these defendants a poisoned chalice is to put it to our lips as well. We must summon such detachment and intellectual integrity that this trial will commend itself to posterity as fulfilling humanity's aspirations to do justice.

The proceedings before the International Military Tribunal lasted more than a year, during which time hundreds of witnesses were heard and thousands of documents — captured by the Allied armies or found in German archives — were received in evidence. The courtroom was open to the world. The accused — who were responsible for the worst atrocities ever perpetrated on the face of the earth — were given "the kind of a trial which they in the days of their pomp and power, never gave to any man."

The court confirmed that the Charter on which the proceedings were based was not an arbitrary exercise of power by the victors but was "the expression of international law existing at the time of its creation; and to that extent is itself a contribution to international law." The argument that the Tribunal was imposing *ex post facto* law was rebutted by the explanation that the maxim *nullem crimen sine lege, nulla poena sine lege* was a general principle of justice that no one should be punished if he could not know at the time that what he did was criminal. The Tribunal upheld the principle but since the convicted men all held high positions and "must have known that they were acting in defiance of all international law when in complete deliberation they carried out their designs of invasion and aggression," there was no injustice in holding them to personal account. The Tribunal cited many existing treaties that had outlawed war, and the Hague Conventions which had codified and clarified the rules for the conduct of hostilities. It would, in the view of the judges, have been unjust to allow those responsible for violations to escape merely because no one had been charged with such offenses in the past. "The law is not static," said the Court, "but by continued adaptation follows the needs of a changing world."

A quadripartite occupation law, Control Council Law No. 10, authorized each occupying power to bring other German war criminals to trial "before an appropriate tribunal." Twelve additional war crimes trials were held in Nuremberg subsequent to the first trial before the IMT. Although these trials were under American auspices, the courts —having been created by multinational law and bound to apply international law — were properly regarded as international courts. The decisions of these subsequent Nuremberg Tribunals served to clarify and create additional precedents of international penal law.

In 1946, an International Military Tribunal for the Far East (IMTFE) was established in Tokyo pursuant to a Charter that was similar to the London Charter for the IMT. Eleven judges from countries with which Japan had been at war heard charges against high-ranking Japanese defendants. The proceedings lasted over two and a half years and it was the biggest trial in recorded history. Although there were dissenting opinions regarding some of the findings of law and the severity of the sentences, the Tokyo Tribunal was another example of the use of international courts as a means of punishing and deterring international crimes.

The Nuremberg and Tokyo Tribunals were the first international criminal courts. Surely, it would have been preferable if both prosecution and judgment had not been by nationals of victor nations over vanguished foes. But, as Justice Jackson pointed out, the worldwide scope of Nazi crimes left few nations really neutral. Those who favored an international criminal court had never suggested that such a tribunal should serve as a mask of justice to hide the face of vengeance. Nor was it conceived as a judicial instrument to guard and maintain the *status quo* in a changing world. It was intended to put the world on clear notice that aggression was an international crime and that inhumane acts that shocked the conscience of mankind could be legally prosecuted as crimes against humanity. Offenders, no matter how high their rank, would be treated no better than ordinary criminals. It was a significant reaffirmation that even Decision-Makers were responsible to law. The principles of international penal justice and the trial procedures that emerged from the Nuremberg proceedings were enormous improvements when compared with what had happened after World War I. Nuremberg became a stepping stone for later efforts to codify international criminal law and set the stage for later deliberations regarding the creation of a permanent international criminal court. The Nuremberg principles of law also became the foundation upon which a new code of offenses that jeopardized the peace and security of mankind might be built.

While the war crimes trials were being prepared, other efforts were being made to strengthen the judicial process. It was necessary to resume the work that had been carried on by the Permanent Court of International Justice at the Hague before the events of war had forced it to close its doors. At the same time that the U.N. Charter was being adopted, a Statute for a new World Court — the International Court of Justice (ICJ) — was also formulated; both went into effect on October 24, 1945. The ICJ Statute became part of the U.N. Charter and all U.N. members became parties to it automatically. That did not mean, however, that the Court was given jurisdiction over all disputes. Although, technically, the ICJ was not the legal successor to the PCIJ — which was established outside the framework of the League — continuity of the international court was assured by honoring the declarations made under the optional clause of the old PCIJ statute, and by adopting similar rules for the new or reformed judicial body.

Most states have been unwilling to submit themselves to the compulsory jurisdiction of the World Court. Communist states have argued that it would be an unacceptable infringement on their national sovereignty. The United States, and many others, have accepted the Court's jurisdiction in principle, but by specific reservations have excluded matters which the states themselves regard as falling exclusively within their own domain. Almost fifty states have agreed, under the optional clause, to accept the Court's authority to some extent. The inability of the ICJ to function more effectively is partly attributable to the uncertainty of international law itself and to the mistrust that still prevails among many nations. Although the U.N. Charter (Article 94) gives the Security Council authority to take whatever measures it deems necessary to give effect to the judgments of the ICJ, in practice, the Council — divided by ideology and stymied by the veto power — has failed to discharge that Charter obligation. The shortcomings of the ICJ illustrate the connection between codification, courts and enforcement and the dependence of one upon the other.

On a regional level, the effective use of judicial proceedings has been much more impressive and is much more promising. The best example is the Court of Justice of the European Community (CJEC). Its ten judges — one from each member state — have their seat in Luxemburg. Since the Court began functioning in 1952 (originally as a court of the European Coal and Steel Community,) over 2000 cases have been dealt with, some 1500 judgments have been rendered and they continue to be issued at the rate of about 150 per annum, engaging the services of a staff of some 450 officials. All the member states of the European Community automatically subjected themselves to the compulsory jurisdiction of the CJEC regarding all disputes that might arise under the treaties establishing the Common Market and the European Atomic Energy Community. Although there is no specific enforcement machinery against states, judgments against individuals and corporate entities are enforced via the domestic legal procedures of each member. As the Court gradually built up an impressive body of judicial interpretations and precedents there has been a slow erosion of national authority in favor of community law. Decisions of the CJEC have been honored and implemented. The judgments of this international court have helped to avoid the type of economic conflict which, in the past, frequently served as a stimulus for war.

Another encouraging example of the strengthening of the judicial process can be found in the emergence of Courts of Human Rights in different parts of the world. Following the adoption by the General Assembly of the Universal Declaration of Human Rights on December 10, 1948, a Convention for the Protection of Human Rights and Fundamental Freedoms was signed by a number of European states. It called for the creation of a European Court of Human Rights. A preliminary screening Commission was set up to receive complaints from any person or non-governmental organization claiming to be a victim of a violation of the Convention. The Commission was authorized to resolve the dispute or refer to it a Council of Ministers, which — if no solution could be found — could submit the case for final decision to the Court of Human Rights. The High Contracting Parties undertook to honor the judgments of the Court. These institutions, which are located in Strasbourg, France, have developed a flourishing practice and their decisions have gained increasing respect as they help to protect individual human rights in western Europe.

The inspiring example of the European Court of Human Rights led to the creation of a similar institution on the American continent. An American Convention on Human Rights entered into force in 1978. An Inter-American Commission on Human Rights and an Inter-American Court of Human Rights (modeled on the European pattern) were to assure that the human rights obligations spelled out in the Convention would be honored. The Court, which has its permanent seat in Costa Rica, has only such jurisdiction as is bestowed upon it by the parties. Since this new judicial agency is still in its infancy, it is too early to judge its effectiveness, but its very existence is an encouraging development. In January, 1984, the Andean Group (Bolivia, Colombia, Ecuador, Peru and Venezula) inaugurated a common Court of Justice — which is another manifestation of the trend to turn to judicial proceedings as a means of resolving problems that might otherwise lead to conflict.

A large number of specialized international agencies in such areas as banking, health, labor, trade and atomic energy are also developing adjudicative procedures for settling disputes. The International Monetary Fund, the International Bank for Reconstruction and Development, the International Labor Organization, the International Civil Aviation Organization, the Food and Agriculture Organization of the U.N., the World Health Organization, the International Atomic Energy Agency and the Universal Postal Union are among the many international entities that have, in recent times, worked out and accepted elaborate rules, regulations and verification techniques for resolving differences among members. Nations as far removed from each other as Africa and Latin America have agreed to accept the jurisdiction of the International Centre for the Settlement of Investment Disputes and to enforce its awards immediately.

Proposals are even being considered for an international court to resolve problems relating to outer-space and the evironment. The Law of the Sea provisions for the peaceful settlement of disputes may be the highest point in the development of the judicial process as a means of resolving conflict. It provides that if the parties do not elect to go before the ICJ at the Hague, or to binding arbitration, the dispute must be taken to a (not yet formed) International Tribunal or a Sea-Beds Dispute Settlement Chamber whose decisions are binding. Although certain conflicts affecting "vital interests" may be excluded, it has been pointed out by Professor Sohn that 90% of the treaty provisions are subject to mandatory peaceful adjudication. For the first time, the Soviet bloc accepted an international system for compulsory dispute settlement. The American delegate confirmed: "The importance of this unprecedented achievement in a major global convention cannot be emphasized too strongly." A world record was set for the number of signatures affixed to the treaty on the first day it was opened for signature. Even among those few states that refused to sign (including the United States, Japan, West Germany and Britain,) the new dispute settlement procedures were deemed to be generally acceptable.

Seen in its totality, it is quite clear that the international community has been increasing its acceptance of the judicial process as an effective means of coping with a growing number of problems that might otherwise lead to international conflict: During the past few decades, international tribunals have been used to punish war criminals and condemn aggression as well as crimes against humanity; the World Court has dealt effectively with a considerable number of issues; the Court of Justice of the European Communities has become a flourishing institution; multi-national Courts of Human Rights and related human rights agencies have become a reality; dozens of international organizations have adopted administrative procedures to resolve differences, and finally, the Law of the Sea Treaty — that has been almost universally approved — has developed an elaborate and refined system for dispute settlement by peaceful means. Despite occasional blips and blemishes, and the hesitation of important and powerful states, the record shows a strengthening of the judicial process that should lend encouragement to all objective observers of the historical trend.

III. International Law Enforcement

Enforcement of law without the use of force has been one of the most persistent challenges facing the international community. We have postulated that effective enforcement requires several supporting components: A. An improved international order; B. Arms control; C. Coordinated sanctions backed by an international military force, and D. Social justice. Progress in achieving each of these goals can best be detected if one scans the changes that have taken place over the years.

A. AN EVOLVING INTERNATIONAL ORDER

Six tapestries adorn the halls of the Palace of Nations in Geneva. They tell the story of man's aspirations and progress toward an improved structure of international society. The artists depict the evolution of social life from the family to the clan, the village, the feudal estate, the national state, and — finally — to a universal federation in which peoples of all races are joined together in a circle of peace. In the course of some six thousand years of recorded history, humankind has slowly been moving toward that sublime ideal. Our historical span will note the progression from the earlies times to the feudal period, to the origins of the present system of nation-states, to the "Grand Designs" of philosophers, to the creation of the League of Nations, the United Nations and, finally, the current period of regionalism and expanding international cooperation.

The inadequacy of the monarchic and church systems was underscored by the Thirty-Years War which was brough to an end by the Treaties of Westphalia, around 1648. The war-weary combatants agreed to realign Europe into a pluralistic and secular society of many sovereign and independent states defined by precise borders. Peace was to be assured by a balance of power among potential rivals, who, uncertain of victory, would (theoretically) recognize that avoidance of conflict would be in their own self-interest. The Westpahlian system of independent sovereign nations was the foundation stone for the territorial organization of the world as we know it today. Experience would prove that it was a very weak reed on which to rest humankind's hopes for peace.

Visions of an improved structure of international society filled the minds of many thinkers. An early plan was put forward in 1306 by a French lawyer, Pierre Dubois, who urged the creation of a universal Christian federation headed by the Pope and ruled by a Council of prelates and nobles who could settle disputes among feuding sovereigns. Enforcement would be assured by the combined armies of the Council members. At the beginning of the 17th century, the King of France also proposed a new system of international cooperation. It has become known as Henry IV's Grand Design, but was actually the work of his Foreign Minister, who borrowed the ideas of earlier authors. He advocated that fifteen European states form a union to maintain order in matters of religion, politics and commerce — the issues that most frequently led to wars. A General Council would serve as the united sovereign or court of arbitration; with power to tax and raise an army.

In 1693, William Penn, founder of the Quaker colony in Pennsylvania, wrote an essay calling for the establishment of a European Parliament. Improving on Henry IV's Grand Design, he proposed proportional representation to compensate for differences is the size and wealth of nations. Protection of the weak would be guaranteed by requiring two-thirds consent for new legislation; joint enforcement by all the sovereign members would compel compliance. In England, another Quaker, John Bellers, suggested an annual Congress of European States to agree upon rules necessary to maintain international peace which could be enforced by the combined strength of all. He proposed that Europe be divided into a hundred equal cantons, each of which would send one member to a European Senate, and one additional member for every thousand men or equivalent made available to a standing army or navy which would enforce the parliamentary laws.

The proposals by Penn in America and Bellers in England were resoundingly echoed in France by the Abbé de Saint Pierre, who, in 1713, published a comprehensive *Project for Perpetual Peace in Europe*. Anyone refusing to join the union would be treated as an enemy of peace. Complaints of one sovereign against another would be settled by the Senate and anyone refusing to abide by its judgment would face war by the entire group. The aggressor would also have to forfeit his country and pay reparations. The Abbot's plan provided for inspection and verification, and if a sovereign broke the peace he would be punished —together with two hundred of his ministers! The French philosopher, Jean Jacques Rousseau, a great admirer of the Abbott, wrote: "If . . . this project is chimerical, it is because men are crazy and because to be sane in the midst of madmen is a sort of folly."

The most prominent German philosopher of the time did not consider it folly to pursue the goal of perpetual peace through a world federation of independent states. Immanuel Kant, in his little pamphlet *On Perpetual Peace,* written in 1795, argued that national armies should be abolished. since to compel soldiers to kill or to be killed was a violation of the rights of man. He proposed that free states form a federation under a constitution that would prohibit all wars and safeguard human rights. "A war of extermination," he wrote, "in which the destruction of both parties and of all justice can result, would permit perpetual peace only in the vast burial ground of the human race." Similar ideas were expressed by Jeremy Bentham, who called for a Common Legislature of European States, an International Court of Judicature, disarmament and the emancipation of colonies.

Peace-loving thinkers had been searching for an improved international system that could eliminate the wars that continued to ravage Europe, yet, as we have noted, it was in the fertile soil of the American continent that the seeds of their thought took root. Tom Paine, an Englishman in America, rallied his compatriots to use their "Common Sense" and declare their freedom from the British crown. The culminating triumph of centuries of evolutionary development toward a more rational world order (based on a Congress of states, a common legislature and a Supreme Court) was the formation of a great new nation — The United States of America

At the turn of the 19th century, European states were not ready to accept any new form of international organization — desiring stability they were blind to the need for change. The "Grand Designs" of philosophers, jurists and statesmen were ignored. Decision-Makers would come to re-think their negative positions after the people who depended upon them for protection had endured the tragedies and horrors of the First World War. By the time that war came to its end, the survivors were demanding a new structure of international society where the recurrence of violent conflict among nations would be prevented forever. The "Grand Designs" that had not been taken very seriously in the past, finally attracted widespread public support and acclaim. Literally thousands of peace organizations and their supporters all over the world cried out for the creation of a League of Nations.

President Wilson played an active part in formulating the constitution of the proposed new international organization. The Covenant was the product of political compromise, and, as in all consensus agreements, the most conservative views prevailed. The Assembly of the League was not a place where the collective will could be ascertained and carried out — it was merely a forum where the unanimous consent of the participants might be solicited. In any matter of substance, neither the Assembly nor the Council could act unless all agreed. War was not outlawed but only delayed until certain prescribed procedures (hopefully leading to a resolution of the conflict) were tried. No agreement could be reached on disarmament or the control of arms production — even though they were both specifically recognized as being important if peace was to be secure.

Despite these omissions, the League of Nations must be seen as another significant landmark in man's effort to create an improved structure of international society. For the first time, it established a permanent organization where many states of the world could meet to discuss problems that might jeopardize peace. It established agreed procedures for coping with issues of common concern. The Covenant outlined the measures needed for the security and improvement of the human condition.

The high hopes for the new world organization received a devastating setback when a minority of U.S. Senators succeeded in blocking the two-thirds vote required to ratify the Treaty of Versailles which embraced the Covenant. The feeling of world solidarity received a death blow from the recalcitrancy of the very state which had done more than all others to set up the first League of Nations. The accomplishments of the League during its brief life-span need not be recounted here. Although the League had been a big step forward and though it played a useful role during its early years in resolving important border disputes, its inadequacies became very apparent as nations hesitated or refused to honor the spirit behind the Covenant. By 1939, the idea of collective security had been abandoned without ever having been given a chance. It was not the League that failed the nations but the nations which failed the League. What was lacking was the political will on the part of powerful states that were not prepared to try a new system. Nations began again, as they had in the past, to scramble for military alliances — based on politics or ideology — that they hoped might save them if war came. It was a futile pursuit. War came again — a second World War — with even greater fury. Once more nations would have to look for an improved order of international society to sustain humankind's desperate hope for a more enduring peace.

A proposed Charter for a United Nations Organization was drafted in the summer of 1944 at "Dumbarton Oaks" — a private estate in Washington D.C. Carved in stone, on a wall facing the garden, was the prophetic motto: *"Quod Severis Metes"* — As Ye Sow, so Shall Ye Reap. U.S. Secretary of State Cordell Hull had informed the invited representatives of Britain, China, and the Soviet Union that what was needed was an organization for the "peaceful settlement of international disputes and for the joint use of force, if necessary, to suppress threats to the peace or breaches of the peace." Within a few weeks, the "Big Four" reached agreement on a proposal that could be presented to the victorious allied nations that were about to be assembled at San Francisco to vote upon the new structure of international society.

The proposed new Charter was, an improvement on the Covenant. To begin with, the membership of the new organization would be substantially enlarged — which would help overcome one of the League's major handicaps. A special Economic and Social Council (ECOSOC) would be created to devote itself exclusively to fostering human rights and fundamental freedoms. Furthermore, the General Assembly could pass resolutions by majority vote, and did not require unanimity — as had been the practice under the League. The Security Council would be able to investigate disputes and recommend terms of settlement — it did not, as under the Covenant, have to wait for war to erupt. If the Council decided that a threat to the peace existed, it could order appropriate measures including diplomatic and economic sanctions as well as action by land, sea and air forces. Members would be obliged to make military contingents available, although they could request amelioration of undue burdens. A Military Staff Committee was to guide the Council on military matters, and self-defense against an armed attack would have to be reported promptly and halted as soon as the Council could intervene.

Still, the Dumbarton Oaks proposal did not go far enough. The General Assembly would remain primarily a forum for public discussion, without legislative authority. The question of an international court was deferred. ECOSOC would have only advisory functions. Enforcement by the Security Council would be dependent upon military contingents to be mustered pursuant to some future agreement — that might never be reached. And, — most vital of all — Council action was to be subject to an absolute veto by any one of the five Permanent Members (U.S., U.K., U.S.S.R., China and France). From the outset, both the Soviet Union and the United States had taken the position that enforcement measures could only be authorized with the concurrence of those states that were expected to carry the brunt of the responsibility. Roosevelt had promised Stalin that the peace of the world would be maintained by the "Four Policemen," and that the "Big Four" would act only by unanimous consent. The U.S. President, a political realist, knew that the American public, weary of war and flushed with the pride of victory, would not agree to any new system that might require American servicemen to face combat overseas without the prior consent of their own government. The Soviet's surely felt the same way. Any other response at that time would have required a degree of vision, courage and leadership that would have been unreasonable to expect.

The insufficiencies of the Dumbarton Oaks proposals did not go unnoticed at San Francisco. But, it might have been seen as base ingratitude had any of the liberated countries offered a serious challenge to the plan so meticulously prepared by those who had brought home the fruits of victory. In the end, with only relatively minor modifications, the proposals were accepted and the U.N. Charter was adopted. The U.S. Secretary of State reported:

What has resulted is a human document with human

imperfections, but with human hopes and human victory as well. But whatever its imperfections, the Charter . . . offers the world an instrument by which a real beginning may be made upon the work of peace.

Without unanimity among the Permanent Members of the Security Council it would be impossible to carry out the security plan of the Charter. It soon appeared that the ideological feud between the Soviet Union and the United States — coupled with the veto power that each possessed — would bring the Council to a virtual stalemate. Weak states were at the mercy of the strong ones. In their search for security, and to meet the needs of a changing society that was growing increasingly complex, smaller nations in particular were driven toward regional coalitions based on mutual economic, religious, political or other interests. This clear movement towards regionalism became another indication of the evolutionary movement in the direction of a more rational world order.

It was in 1948 that the Organization of American States (OAS) was formed. Its early origins can be traced back to 1881 when, on U.S. initiative, several Latin nations began to meet to consider mutual legal, economic and political problems, but it was only after the second world war that these efforts reached fruition. A conference of seven independent African states was convened in 1958 and, by 1963, it was possible for thirty-two African leaders to form the Organization of African Unity (OAU). Of course, these are fragile beginnings and the environmental, economic and political problems they face are enormous, but it does represent a serious effort to make international society more responsive to the needs of its human inhabitants.

Western Europe, the scene of countless wars and the cradle of two world conflagrations is in the forefront of the movement toward an integrated community of states. Despite past feuds and linguistic barriers, west European states are determined to trade, work and live together in peaceful brotherhood. In 1979, the ten Common Market countries — with distinctive cultures and traditions — elected a European Parliament. Like every infant, it was limited in its efficiency and capability, but the important fact was that it came into existence. Another advance in the structure of world organization!

Regional cooperation and organization has become a fact of life all over the globe. Not all associations have yet reached the level of the European community with its parliament, courts and enforcement mechanisms that we have mentioned, but the inclination and the need to move in that direction is clear. Arab states have, during recent years, increased their cooperation for various economic or political purposes. The League of Arab States has twenty-two members and the Islamic Council has forty-two members. Cooperation among Nordic states is being encouraged by multinational treaties calling for expanded collaboration in juridical, cultural, social and economic fields. The Association of South-East Asian Nations (ASEAN) was formed in 1967 to stimulate economic and social cooperation among five states in the Pacific region. Many small states have associated themselves in unions of various kinds to enhance their common interests. Developing countries have formed a "Group of 77," while over a hundred nations have belied their title by aligning themselves as a Group of Non-Aligned" states to protect their common political interests.

Furthermore, a host of international organizations and specialized agencies, both governmental and non-governmental, have improved the functioning of the international order in hundreds of ways that were inconceivable not too long ago. The International Atomic Energy Agency, proposed by President Dwight Eisenhower in 1953, from its headquarters in Vienna, promotes and controls the peaceful uses of nuclear energy in over a hundred countries. An International Maritime Organization, with over 120 members and headquarters in London, seeks to improve maritime safety and prevent maritime pollution. The U.N. Conference on Trade and Development (UNCTAD) is located in Geneva; it aims to promote world-wide trade. The International Air Transport Association, established in Montreal, regulates the airlines of many nations. The World Health Organization operates out of regional offices in various parts of the world. A U.N. Environmental Program is stationed in Nairobi. A World Meteorological Organization, acting through six regional associations, monitors and reports on weather conditions. There is effective international coordination in the fields of broadcasting and telecommunications. Even outer-space is beginning to be governed by binding international agreements; a 1967 treaty stipulates that outer-space, including the moon and other celestial bodies, shall be the province of all mankind. Agreements exist for the rescue of astronauts and for determining liability for injuries caused by space objects. The Law of the Sea regulates a broad range of issues regarding about four-fifths of the surface of Planet Earth. Within recent memory, the land, the seas and the skies have become objects of increasing international cooperation.

From our scan of humankind's efforts to improve the functioning of the international order as a means of preserving peace, we see that despite the "Grand Designs" of leading thinkers, it was war itself — and the shock of its horrors — that became the principal stimulus for progress. The Thirty-Years War produced the Peace of Westphalia in 1648. The Napoleonic Wars gave birth to the Congress of Vienna, in 1815, where the nations that brought down the Emperor bartered territories and agreed to consult on future peace problems. The threat of war and the burden of an arms race produced the Hague Conferences of 1899 and 1907. World War I inspired the creation of the League of Nations. The tragedies of the Second World War led to the formation of the United Nations in 1945. The failure of the U.N. to live up to its promise has caused many nations to move toward regionalism and to voluntary acceptance of an elaborate variety of international controls affecting a vast sphere of human activity and endeavor. The number of nations joining in cooperative international efforts has been consistently increasing. Each advance — though inadequate — was an improvement on the past. The line of progress is there for all to see.

B. GROPING TOWARD ARMS CONTROL

The problem of disarmament is the heart of the most vital challenge to the international order. Although the delegates to the disarmament conferences in the Hague unanimously agreed that "the restriction of military charges, which are at present a heavy burden on the world, is extremely desirable," the Decision-Makers were unwilling to accept any legal obligation to reduce the level of their arms. Article 8 of the Covenant of the League declared: "The Members of the League recognize that the maintenance of peace requires the reduction of national armaments to the lowest point consistent with national safety and the enforcement by common action of international obligations." But, in the early 1920's, the uncompromising attitude of national sovereignty still paralyzed League members and prevented implementation of this recognized requirement for peace. After many years of elaborate preparation, a worldwide disarmament conference was convened in 1932. Sixty-four nations were in attendance. France proposed that the most dangerous weapons be set aside to be used only in self-defense or on orders of the League's Council, and that a standing international force be created to make sure that nations carried out the obligations nations were expected to accept in a new Disarmament Convention. The French plan was far ahead of its time. The Disarmament Conference was unable to reach agreement on which weapons were offensive or defensive. While nations were talking disarmament, most of the major powers were, in fact, rearming and preparing for war.

A specific call to produce a plan for the reduction of national arms appeared again when the U.N. Charter was approved in 1945. Article 26 called for the Council to submit a disarmament plan in order to promote the establishment and maintenance of peace with the least possible diversion for armaments of the world's human and economic resources. At its very first meeting, the General Assembly, in its very first resolution, agreed unanimously to create an Atomic Energy Commission to plan the gradual elimination of weapons of mass destruction under a system of safeguards that would prevent violations. The need for disarmament, and particularly the urgent requirement that atomic energy be brought under international control, was clearly recognized by all.

At a time when the United States had a monopoly on nuclear weapons, it was the U.S. which took the initiative in proposing that atomic energy be used solely for peaceful purposes. The details of the American proposal appeared in what came to be known as the "Baruch Plan" — named after the elder statesman who first made it public. He suggested that an International Atomic Development Authority be created with complete control of all atomic energy activities, including a halt in the production of atomic weapons, destruction of existing atomic bombs, and a ban on all future weapons of mass destruction. But before the U.S. would be willing to disclose its secrets and destroy its atomic weapons, two conditions would have to be met: 1- It would be necessary to have a binding agreement on a system of inspection and controls to verify compliance; 2- There would have to be agreement that violators would face criminal prosecution by a Nuremberg-type international tribunal which would not be restricted by any veto power. "Penalization is essential," said Mr. Baruch, "if peace is to be more than a feverish interlude between wars."

The U.S.S.R. had no difficulty in agreeing that existing stockpiles of atomic weapons should be destroyed — presumably the Soviets had none. It was agreed that nuclear weapons should be banned, that scientific information should be exchanged and that violations should be regarded as a crime against humanity — which the Soviets felt could adequately be dealt with by national (rather than international) penal jurisdiction. It was the Soviet view that only the Security Council — with its veto power intact — could decide on sanctions for violations of such an international agreement. The Russians felt that the first step should be to draw up a draft Convention prohibiting atomic weapons. There should then be clarification of the limits of inspection to make sure that it would not interfere with Soviet production in unrelated fields — which the Soviets thought might be a form of espionage. On the main point, the U.S.S.R. agreed: "Strict international control and inspection of atomic energy should be established."

A U.N. Commission for Conventional Armaments was appointed to bring about reductions in non-atomic weapons. In 1949, the Soviets proposed an across-the-board cut of one-third of all the armaments and armed forces of the Permanent Members of the Security Council. The United States rejected the proposal but was prepared to support a French plan that called for an international census of arms as a starting point. Without a clear-cut and binding prior agreement that assured independent inspection and verification of the level of arms and the implementation of agreed measures of reduction, the U.S. was not prepared to reduce or limit its weapons of any kind. Despite the fact that there seemed to be agreement in principle, and both parties clearly recognized that disarmament was desirable and that there must be independent verification and control regarding the reduction of atomic weapons, the degree of suspicion and distrust between the two superpowers was so intense that no agreement could be reached. By 1950, the efforts to control arms were completely stymied.

In 1959, Soviet Premier Nikita Khruschev, speaking at the United Nations, called for a program of general and complete disarmament. The U.S. representative replied that the United States could support such a policy. When John F. Kennedy was elected President in 1960, he appointed John J. McCloy, a former Assistant Secretary of War and a distinguished public servant, to establish an Arms Control and Disarmament Agency and to renew efforts to reach a disarmament agreement with the Soviet Union. McCloy was Chairman of the influential Council on Foreign Relations (a private organization of prominent Americans) and, in 1956, had written in an introduction to a Council publication that the U.S. had to be ready to consider "total disarmament — universal, enforceable and complete." His general attitude on the subject was, therefore, well known and it was consistent with the statement that had been made by the head of the Soviet Union.

Following several meetings in New York, Moscow and Washington, Presidential Advisor McCloy and Soviety Deputy Foreign Minister Valery Zorin were able to agree upon a Joint Statement of Principles. The McCloy-Zorin agreement of September, 1961 recognized that general and complete disarmament was the goal of both nations. The disarmament measures, they agreed, were to be implemented "from beginning to end under such strict and effective international control as would provide firm assurance that all parties are honoring their obligations." Inspectors from an International Disarmament Organization were to have "unrestricted access without veto to all places, as necessary for the purpose of effective verification." Existing armed forces were to be disbanded; stockpiles of weapons of mass destruction were to be eliminated; all military training institutions were to be closed; military expenditures were to be discontinued and the entire disarmament program was to be implemented and verified in specific stages within specified time limits. The planned disarmament measures were not to take place in a vacuum; they were to be accompanied by complementary actions to strengthen institutions for the settlement of international disputes by peaceful means and (as shall be considered later) for the creation of an effective international peace force. It was a completely rational and comprehensive approach to disarmament and absolutely consistent with the principles laid down in both the Covenant of the League and the Charter of the U.N. The McCloy-Zorin plan was promptly hailed by the entire General Assembly of the United Nations.

President Kennedy, addressing the United Nations in 1961, declared:

> Today, every man, woman and child lives under a sword of Damocles, hanging by the slenderest of threads, capable of being cut at any moment. [He challenged the Soviet Union] not to an arms race, but to a peace race: To advance together step by step, stage by stage, until general and complete disarmament has actually been achieved.

The heads of state of the two superpowers had publicly declared before the whole world that they favored general and complete disarmament. It was a remarkable step forward in international relations. But, the solemn declarations failed to be implemented because neither power was able to move decisively away from its traditional concepts of unfetterd national security based on military power. Fear and suspicion remained in control. The Soviets were ready to have their *destruction* of existing arms verified by international inspectors but they were not ready to allow anyone to check their *existing* stockpiles. McCloy insisted that verification of the level of existing arms at every stage of the reduction process was an essential part of the deal. This difference should not have been insurmountable, but on this relatively fine point, the McCloy-Zorin agreement foundered.

Despite the breakdown of the McCloy-Zorin agreement, the two superpowers had come very close to a rational peace accord. Although they did not succeed in 1961, it may be useful to point out some of the positive steps taken in recent years to help reduce the risks of nuclear destruction. Throughout the world, certain "nuclear-free zones" have been established, where testing, use, production or even possession of nuclear weapons is prohibited. The Antarctic Treaty of 1959 —accepted by both the Soviet Union and the United States — provides that "Antarctica shall be used for peaceful purposes only." Outer-space and the moon were given protected status against weapons of mass destruction by a treaty signed in 1967. Nuclear weapons tests in the atmosphere, outerspace and under water were banned in 1963. Latin America, with some 200 million inhabitants, became a nuclear-free zone in 1967, and a special agency was created specifically to monitor compliance. In 1968, a non-proliferation treaty reaffirmed the goal of complete disarmament under international controls, and nuclear states agreed not to transfer their military technology to others. In 1970, the sea-bed was excluded as a base for weapons of mass destruction. Agreements went into effect to cope with nuclear accidents or incidents over the high seas, and "hot-lines" of instant communication were established between the superpowers to help reduce the risks of miscalculation. The United States and the Soviety Union, in 1972, signed and ratified a treaty limiting the anti-ballistic missiles that each country might have, deploy or test, and supplementary restrictions were accepted by both nations when President Richard Nixon met General Secretary Brezhnev in Moscow in 1974. Strategic Arms Limitations Talks (SALT) led to agreements in 1972 and 1979 which restricted the production of certain nuclear arms, and even though the U.S. withheld ratification of the SALT accords, their restraints have generally been honored by both sides. These arms control measures were all positive accomplishments and should not be underrated.

The arms control measures that have already been agreed upon are insufficient to satisfy the declared aspirations of world leaders. (They also fail to meet the obligations of the U.N. Charter.) Still, disarmament negotiations are continuing between the superpowers as well as on a multinational level. Many specific proposals are on the table and the continued debate about these complicated and technical problems holds promise that — in time — solutions will be found — IF and WHEN Decision-Makers are willing to take a chance for peace.

C. SANCTIONS AND AN INTERNATIONAL FORCE

We have seen that the international order is being improved in a large variety of ways and that significant — if inadequate — progress may be detected in the realm of arms control. Powerful nations could hardly be expected to deprive themselves of arms as long as there was no operational alternative for the peaceful settlement of disputes and they could not know in advance what help they would receive from others if they were attacked or what military assistance they might be called upon to render to others in the common defense. The disarray and lack of cohesion in the international order prevented nations from working out an effective system of economic sanctions to maintain the peace. The prevailing mistrust that inhibited nations from reducing their military arsenals also blocked the creation of an adequate international peace force to take the place of national armies.

It was recognized in the Covenant of the League that disarmament and sanctions went hand in hand and were dependent upon each other. Article 16 — the "economic weapon" of the Covenant — provided that if any member went to war unlawfully, all other Members would immediately subject the law breaker to "severance of all trade and financial relations." Boycott and blockade were mandatory and Members promised mutual support in order to minimize the loss and inconvenience resulting from such sanctions. The use of armed might was quite another matter; the Council could only *recommend* what military forces the Members were to contribute in order to protect the Covenant.

Various committees of the League set to work to consider the many problems that would have to be resolved before sanctions without the use of force could be made effective. It soon became apparent that if measures of economic coercion were to serve their purpose, they would have to be applied promptly and comprehensively by all (or most) states acting in a coordinated and collective way. States that were not Members of the League would have to cooperate or run the risk that they too would be blockaded. This created certain hazards and possible hardships that had not been fully anticipated — if small states tried to blockade a powerful neighbor, such hostile action might provoke immediate counter-measures or even an invasion by the aggressor. Poorer nations might face ruinous financial burdens if they had to sever their trade and financial ties with a warring state. An International Blockade Committee was therefore appointed to consider the problem and seek solutions.

A number of resolutions adopted in 1921 showed that many states were most reluctant to bind themselves to take the stringent economic measures necessary to enforce the Covenant. In the end, certain "rules for guidance" were adopted which, in effect, left it to the states themselves to decide whether there had been a breach of the Covenant and when and whether economic sanctions would be applied. Although the obligation was made discretionary, the specific steps that would be required were spelled out: permanent machinery would be needed in order to keep currently informed about the economic relations between different states as well as the financial condition of many nations; domestic legislation would have to be enacted to enable states to take enforcement measures without delay; the rights and duties of non-belligerents required clarification, and many technical problems of import-export controls would have to be overcome. All that was needed was the will to act.

Japan's invasion of Manchuria in 1931 was the first significant challenge to the security system of the League. At that time, the strong powers — upon whom enforcement depended — were in the midst of an economic depression and in no mood to exert coercive economic pressures to preserve a distant empire. Small nations could not undertake the responsibility alone. Japan showed its disdain by withdrawing from the League in 1933. The final epitaph for the world body was written by Italy's war of aggression against Ethiopia in 1936. When Italy went to war against another Member of the League, in clear violation of the Covenant, Article 16 was automatically supposed to go into effect. For the first time, it appeared that nations would be united and international law would be enforced by the collective economic sanctions that were being mobilized. Fifty nations condemned the Italian aggression and hosts of committees began to work on the technical details required to apply the sanctions called for by the Covenant. An embargo on arms to the victim, Ethiopia, was lifted. Lists of vital commodities and resources were prepared. National legislation authorizing the necessary coercive measures was already on the books of many states and was being copied by others. Export licensing and controls, coupled with a system of inspections, fines and other penalties, were ready for prompt implementation. An oil embargo was prepared in order to cripple Italy's war potential. No one doubted that these comprehensive sanctions, rigorously applied, would restore peace.

The main obstacles blocking effective sanctions were not legal or technical — they were political. France and Britian, for their own political purposes, reneged on their promises. Italy's good will was more important to them (as a potential buffer against Germany) than Ethiopia's pathetic pleas for justice. Smaller states realized that they were being asked to make sacrifices for the common good while big powers were continuing to play their old political game. The enforcement measures ground to a halt. Failure to honor the sanctions provisions of the Covenant meant that aggression could not be stopped by peaceful means — and the path was opened for the next World War.

After World War II, it was hoped that nations would learn from the mistakes and omissions of the past. The U.N. Charter provided that if ever there was another threat to the peace, the Security Council could call upon the Members to apply coercive measures, including complete interruption of economic and diplomatic relations as well as the severance of all communications. Should such non-violent means prove inadequate, the Council was authorized by Article 42 to take "such action by air, sea, or land forces as may be necessary to maintain or restore international peace and security." Members obligated themselves to make such forces available on the Council's call — pursuant to agreements which the Members undertook to negotiate as soon as possible. Article 45 provided:

> In order to enable the United Nations to take urgent military measures, Members shall hold immediately available national air-force contingents for combined international enforcement.

The Charter reaffirmed the basic security plan of the Covenant and, for the first time, recognized the need for a combined military force to maintain or restore peace. What they failed adequately to take into account was, as we have noted, that the effectiveness of the security system depended upon unanimity among the major powers. The absence of unanimity, coupled with the veto power, meant that the plan for world security — either by way of economic sanctions or by combined international military force — would not be implemented.

The inability of the Permanent Members of the Security Council to agree on sanctions against those who breached the peace meant that many wars would be waged and the Security Council would be unable to intervene to restore law and order. The United States, often under domestic political pressure to "do something," led measures of economic warfare against nations that it perceived to be jeopardizing world security. Economic controls that were traditional in times of war, became weapons of the "Cold War." "Most-Favored-Nations" (MFN) tariff treatment, for example, was reserved for states that shared or accepted American political and social objectives. Communist China, North Korea, Vietnam, the U.S.S.R., Cuba and Nicaragua were among those subjected to export and import prohibitions, higher duties, blocking of assets, restrictions on currency transactions, credit restraints, travel, shipping and port denials, and — in the case of Nicaragua — even to an alleged blockade and the mining of its harbors. But, American measures of economic coercion were almost invariably more restrictive than those which its allies were willing to impose. Under the circumstances, the impact was less compelling than what was desired by the United States. Other trading partners were available to fill gaps, and target states were driven toward increased mutual dependence and solidarity — without noticeably modifying their objectionable practices.

Even where violations of international law seemed blatant, the world community lacked effective tools for peaceful law enforcement. The invasion of Hungary by Soviet troops in 1956, and their invasion of Czechoslovakia in 1968 (both under the guise of collective self-defense) evoked some international protests but nothing concrete was done to interdict the military *faits accomplis*. When the Soviets invaded Afghanistan in 1980, 104 nations, meeting in an Emergency Session of the U.N., issued a strong rebuke by calling for immediate withdrawal of foreign troops. It was ignored. The U.S. decided to boycott the Olympic games scheduled to be held in Moscow in 1981, and imposed a unilateral grain embargo on the Soviet Union. The games went on without U.S. athletes, and Russia simply bought its grain in other markets, such as Canada, Australia and Argentina. When it was recognized that the embargo penalized U.S. farmers more than it did the Soviets, the U.S. returned to "business as usual." A 1981 embargo on the shipment of parts for the construction of a Soviet pipeline across Europe had to be lifted when it encountered opposition from America's European allies that were partners with the U.S.S.R. The U.S. economic boycott of Cuba and Nicaragua pressed those nations to increase their economic cooperation with the Soviet Union, which made them more dependent upon the U.S.S.R. and that, presumably, ran counter to American interests. Experience showed that a unilateral policy of embargoes, boycotts and trade restraints — even by a very rich and powerful nation — could not be effective to restore peace.

One of the most impressive uses of economic sanctions was an oil embargo imposed in 1973 by the Organization of Petroleum Exporting Countries (OPEC), a cartel that controlled the world oil market. Many industrial nations, faced with a threat to their vital industrial capacity, lost little time in complying with OPEC demands for political pressure on Israel, the real target of the sanctions. The victim states were able to reduce their vulnerability by forming protective associations, lowering oil consumption and launching a massive search for alternate energy sources. Even the use of the "oil weapon" by a number of important suppliers could not be effective for long.

The most extensive sanctions applied since World War II were directed against the government of South Africa for its racial policy of apartheid, which was denounced by the General Assembly as a "crime against humanity." Despite economic sanctions by many nations, some of South Africa's important trading partners (notably, the U.S., U.K., West Germany and France) condemned apartheid but were not willing to join in boycotting a country on which they depended for vital minerals and which was a military friend, if not ally. A U.N. Special Committee, appointed to make sanctions against South Africa more effective, reported in 1982 that its work had been brought to a virtual standstill. What was required — but what was lacking — was a comprehensive organization of the world's resources and a coordinated system to implement and police punitive measures against the transgressor.

The inability of states to implement the Charter security plan regarding effective economic sanctions was matched by the Security Council's inability to reach agreement on the creation of an international force. The Military Staff Committee, created pursuant to Article 47, was expected to submit a disarmament proposal and to present a plan for the creation of the international force envisaged under Article 43. After due deliberation, the Committee proposed that member nations make available national land, sea and air units in sufficient strength to enable the Council to discharge its peacekeeping responsibilities. A report of the Military Staff Committee, in April, 1947, described the general principles that were to govern the establishment of the peace force: its purpose, over-all strength, the contributions by member nations, the conditions and controls that were to apply, its degree of readiness, provisions for assistance, facilities and rights of passage, logistical support and its strategic location and command. The Chiefs of Staff who were represented on the Military Committee reached agreement by consensus on all but sixteen out of the forty-one articles outlining how the proposed international force would operate. The Russians wanted each nation to contribute an equal number of units, whereas the British and Americans wanted greater flexibility. The U.S.S.R. opposed stationing foreign troops on Soviet soil, but these technical differences did not seem fundamental or irreconcilable. Once again, the difficulties were political.

Although the outline of how an international military force could be created was fairly clear, the Military Staff Committee — which continued to meet in perfunctory annual sessions — made no further progress. They were stymied by the dilemma that as long as there was no agreement on disarmament, it was not possible to reach an agreement regarding the size, composition or anything else affecting the international force. Without an international force, no nation would disarm. It was another clear illustration that the Charter security plan was dependent upon all of its components being accepted; everything was intertwined. Nonetheless, progress toward an international peace force was made in ways that none of the framers of the Charter had fully anticipated.

In 1950, with the Soviets absent from the Security Council (in protest against the refusal to seat communist China,) it was possible —for the first time — to create an international military force under U.N. command. U.S. General Douglas MacArthur was in charge of a multinational army assembled to halt aggression by the communist People's Democratic Republic of North Korea against the Republic of Korea in the south. The international force went into action under the U.N. flag flying next to the flag of the participating states. It was not exactly the international force envisioned by the Charter, but it was, in the words of the U.N. Commission, "the first effort to enforce the principles of collective security through a worldwide international organization." After much fighting, hostilities were brought to a halt in 1953. A U.N. Military Armistice Commission still helps to reduce tensions and deter hostilities along the border of that divided land.

The Republic of the Congo received its independence from Belgium in 1960 — only to be faced with an immediate breakdown of law and order as competing tribes and provinces scrambled for power. Belgian troops were landed (to protect Belgian interests) in mineral-rich Katanga province which declared itself an independent state. Heavy fighting ensued. The Security Council agreed to provide the Congo government with "such military assistance as may be necessary" until the Republic's own forces could discharge their responsibilities. A

United Nations Force (ONUC — Opération des Nations Unies au Congo) was quickly assembled by Secretary-General Dag Hammarskjold to help avert all-out civil war. The Security Council authorized him to "use the requisite measure of force" to expel foreign military personnel not under U.N. command. In 1963, when U.N. forces were fired upon, they counter-attacked, defeated the insurgents and put an end to the secession. This action by U.N. Forces in the Congo created a significant precedent: a U.N. military force had been assembled, it had undertaken a humanitarian task and had intervened to protect the territorial integrity and independence of a new African state. It had restored law and order and had expelled hostile foreign troops from the country. Despite sporadic recurrence of hostilities, an international military force created by and under the command of the United Nations had been used effectively for law enforcement and the restoration of peace.

For many years, the Greek community on the island of Cyprus has been striving to form a union with Greece. The militant Turkish minority on the island seeks an alignment with Turkey. In 1963, a British, Greek and Turkish peacekeeping force helped to restore peace between warring factions. When these measures proved inadequate, the Security Council — by unanimous vote — organized and deployed a U.N. Force in Cyprus (UNFICYP) and appointed a U.N. Mediator. UNFICYP has had its mandate periodically renewed, and the multinational army acting under Security Council control continues to play an important peacekeeping role on the island.

U.N. peacekeeping forces have also played a significant part in tamping down the fires of conflict in the Middle East. In 1956, a U.N. Truce Supervision Organization (UNTSO) was created to monitor a truce in the area. A U.N. Emergency Force (UNEF) of some six thousand men from ten nations was moved into the Suez region as British, French and Israeli troops — under pressure from both the United States and the Soviet Union — were persuaded to withdraw. Although the formation of that international force was ordered by the General Assembly — which was not the procedure prescribed by the Charter — U.S. President Eisenhower reported: "The first truly international peace force has been created and was playing a vital role in maintaining peace in a troubled area." An army created by the Assembly (rather than the Security Council) could only be stationed on foreign soil with the consent of the sovereign state. A police force that could be sent packing when violence might erupt could hardly be effective — as subsequent events would show. In May, 1967, Egypt ordered the removal of all U.N. Forces and closed the Gulf of Aqaba and the Strait of Tiran to Israel shipping. Israel, fearing an imminent attack by Egypt, launched a preemptive strike. The Security Council — by unanimous vote — demanded a cease-fire. Within six days, the fighting was again brought to a halt. It was quite obvious that if the superpowers were in agreement, less powerful states would simply have to comply with their demands.

The persuasive power of overwhelming military might was once again demonstrated in the "Day of Atonement War" that erupted in 1973 when Egypt and Syria launched surprise attacks against Israel. When Israel regained the initiative, the Soviet Union massed its own forces and prepared to rescue the beleaguered Arab armies. Oil-producing states threatened to cut off all oil supplies to any state supporting Israel. In response, U.S. Secretary of State Henry Kissinger met in urgent session with Soviet Chairman Brezhnev and together they drafted U.N. resolutions that brought a halt to the fighting and the appointment of the U.N. Emergency Force (UNEF) to monitor the front between Egypt and Israel. A U.N. Disengagement Observer Force (UNDOF) was created in 1974 to monitor the Israel-Syrian border, and its mandate has been regularly renewed. A U.N. Interim Force in Lebanon (UNIFIL), consisting of about seven thousand men from fifteen nations, was created in 1975 to serve as a buffer in the area. These limited efforts were not adequate to bring peace to the explosive and fanatical conflicts of the Middle East and other multinational forces (organized by the U.S. France, Italy and England) also failed to achieve their ultimate goals. But they all reflected a developing trend toward the growth of international military force to maintain peace.

As we scan the movement from the first international force to fly the U.N. flag in Korea in 1950, to the many subsequent formations of international military units: in the Congo, Cyprus, Egypt, Syria and Lebanon, there can be little doubt that such multinational forces — relying more on armbands than on arms — have shown what an international military force adequately organized and manned would be able to do to restore or maintain peace — if they were given a fair chance.

D. EMERGING SOCIAL JUSTICE

It has been recognized since the time of Cicero and Grotius that social justice and peace go hand in hand. It is common sense that people are more likely to obey rules if they are convinced that the restraints or regulations are generally reasonable and equitable. The Covenant of the League made reference to the need for fair and humane conditions of labor and called for the just treatment of inhabitants of colonial territories — but these humanitarian appeals were inserted at the end as almost casual afterthoughts. The U.N. Charter, by contrast, in its Preamble expressed the determination of the organization to maintain justice, promote social progress and better standards of life in larger freedom and "to employ international machinery for the promotion of the economic and social advancement of all peoples." The fundamental purpose of the organization was declared to be the settlement of disputes by peaceful means and in conformity with the principles of "justice and international law." The promotion of human rights and the collective solution of economic and social problems was — for the first time — accepted as a principal goal of international society, and the Economic and Social Council (ECOSOC) was charged with primary responsibility for recommending economic, cultural, educational, health and other social improvements.

International concern for human rights is one of the great emergent historical forces of our time. From ancient Greek and Roman concepts about the natural rights of man there has emerged the gradual codification of bills of rights designed to guarantee individual liberty and well being. The *Magna Carta* of 1215 prohibited punishment except by law and the judgment of one's peers. American and French revolutions were fought to protect the rights of the common man. Constitutions enacted during the 19th and 20th centuries expressed their concern for human rights. Even in warfare, the laws of humanity were to be respected. The Covenant of the League elevated the welfare of man to the international level and the Charter of the U.N. was even more explicit. It inspired a host of human rights instruments and agencies whose activities span the globe. One can hardly imagine the chaos and increased suffering that would exist in the world today were it not for the cooperative actions taken during the past few decades to bring about a more equitable distribution of social advantages.

An alphabet of acronyms is needed to abbreviate the names of new international agencies now coping with problems of social justice. The path was first marked by the International Labor Organization (ILO) created after World War I to establish fair labor standards everywhere. In the sphere of economics, the U.N. Conference on Trade and Development (UNCTAD), created in 1964, regularly brings together well over 150 states to coordinate policies for both developed and developing countries. Restrictive trade barriers have been dismantled, commodity distribution has been improved and the industrial capacity of developing nations has been strengthened. The General Agreement on Tariffs and Trade (GATT), the U.N. Commission on International Trade Law (UNCITRAL), the International Fund for Agricultural Development (IFAD), the International Monetary Fund (IMF), the International Bank for Reconstruction and Development (IBRD), the U.N. Development Programs (UNDP) and the U.N. Industrial Development Organization (UNIDO) are among the very many multinational institutions now seeking to improve the lot of the underprivileged.

In the decade of the 1960's and 1970's, global development strategies were inaugurated. By 1974, nations were beginning to work on a Charter of Economic Rights and Duties of States and on the establishment of a New International Economic Order (NIEO). The efforts to master the world's monetary problems, provide development loans, regulate practices of multinational corporations, eliminate trade barriers and clarify norms of international economic behavior are illustrative of the growing movement toward comprehensive economic cooperation on a regional and world-wide level. It was Ambassador Arvid Pardo of the tiny island of Malta who, at the General Assembly of 1967, gave expression to the inspiring dream that untapped resources of the ocean should be used for the benefit of those most in need, for it was part of the "common heritage of mankind." Since man first began to explore outer-space, it has been recognized that the heavens should be used for the benefit of all. The 1967 Treaty on Principles Governing the Activities of States in the Exploration and Use of Outer-Space, Including the Moon and Other Celestial Bodies, specifically states that outer-space "shall be the province of all mankind." Professor Carl Q. Christol of the University of Souther California, noting that the principle of "common use" was supported by both President Dwight Eisenhower and the U.N. General Assembly, has concluded that there is increasing evidence that states must view their options from the perspective of an existing world community: "A too heavy reliance on certain national-interest policies may be counterproductive and regrettably myopic." Most nations have come to accept the idea that all of humankind should be the beneficiary of the wealth that lies in the ocean, beneath the seas, on the moon and in outer-space. The surface of the earth is only a very small portion of the enormous area which is already dedicated to the betterment of humankind. Can the remaining tiny fraction be far behind?

Of course, there are still dictatorial régimes, and of course, people are still persecuted all over the world, and there are millions of refugees seeking their fair share of humanity. But what is remarkable and noteworthy in the present context is that there are substantial and increasing efforts being made on a global and cooperative basis to eliminate or diminish what are now generally recognized to be evil and intolerable conditions. The European Convention on Human Rights of 1950, and a similar 1969 Convention for Latin America are being implemented, as we have noted, by Courts of Human Rights. The African Charter on Human and People's Rights of 1981 is beginning to influence some African states. The individual has, in the words of Professor Lauterpacht of Cambridge, been transformed from "an object of international compassion to a subject of international rights." Some nations may still persecute their own citizens — but no longer can they say that it is nobody's business but their own!

It has been noted that in recent years "the problem of human welfare is a single process which transcends all distinctions of race, creed, colour, national origin, social and economic status and all national boundaries and ideological affiliation." Education for human rights is a world-wide and ongoing process, in which the United Nations plays a very important role. Many non-governmental organization, such as Amnesty International, the International Commission of Jurists and church groups of all denominations are dedicated to the global protection of human rights. As has been noted by the distinguished Professor Myres McDougal of Yale, "the world community is moving toward an ever more powerful consensus on the basic components of an international bill of rights." Continuing education for human rights is an essential process that has been steadily growing throughout the world. As international concern for the fundamental rights of all human beings continues to expand, the idea moves ever closer to fulfillment.

The activities of the World Health Organization (WHO) must also be appreciated. Malaria and smallpox have all but been eliminated from the face of the earth. Other infectious diseases are being controlled, infant mortality has been reduced significantly and life expectancy has been raised. WHO's membership is universal. Its secretariat is composed of more than five thousand scientific and administrative persons and its budget is about $500 million per annum. Its goal is "the attainment by all peoples of the highest possible level of health." In the process of helping to improve the health of human beings in many neglected areas of the world, it has contributed not only to social justice but to the maintenance of peace and stability as well.

Increased efficiency in the production and distribution of food, resulting from the efforts by the Food and Agriculture Organization (FAO) — another specialized agency of the U.N. — has raised the level and the standards of nutrition in many regions of deprivation. The FAO was created in 1945 to help ensure humanity's freedom from hunger. Its scientific research regarding food, agriculture, fishing and forestry has helped to increase food production and to define standards of nutrition. Other U.N. programs and commissions deal with problems of housing the least advantaged. Cooperative international measures help to protect the physically handicapped, to safeguard social insurance benefits and to further the rights of women. The United Nations Children's Fund (UNICEF) has drawn attention to the special needs of children. Measures for the protection of the environment are also receiving increasing national and international attention.

The dissolution of the colonial system during the past few decades was another manifestation of world recognition that all peoples are entitled to equal dignity. Other measures of social justice include the many multinational efforts to reduce illiteracy and to make education more available to the underprivileged. International programs seek to control and prevent crime, to set minimum standards for the treatment of prisoners and to curtail the use of narcotic drugs. The U.N. High Commissioner for Refugees, aided by regional organizations and many multinational church and welfare groups, has ameliorated the sufferings of refugees, stateless persons and those seeking territorial asylum. By 1984, the United States held membership in over one hundred international organizations aimed at improving the human condition.

The great advances that have been mentioned should not imply that suffering and poverty have been eradicated — they have not. Perhaps the greatest factor inhibiting greater enhancement of social justice has been the population explosion — from 2.5 billion people in 1950 to 4.7 billion by 1983. Over one billion people have been added to the world population since 1970. The need for population control was recognized and a Population Commission was created by ECOSOC. India and the U.N. jointly established an International Institute for Population Studies, in 1957. Regional training and population research centers for Latin America were established in Santiago in 1957, in Cairo in 1963, in Africa in 1972 and in Bucharest in 1974. A World Population

Conference adopted a comprehensive plan of action, assisted by the U.N. Fund for Population Activities. These cooperative international efforts, as well as the activities of many non-governmental organizations, influenced national policies and practices so that a deceleration of population growth has been made possible in several regions. The inability to stabilize the number of persons in the world has meant that, despite the social improvements mentioned, the gap in the quality of life between rich and poor, black and white, north and south, has not yet been closed. In some respects, it may even be widening. The absence of unanimity within the international community has also diminished the effectiveness of measures taken to close the gap. These shortcomings continue to present great challenges to the world community — particularly to the more powerful and wealthy nations — but they do not detract from the undeniable fact that more progress has been made in recent years than ever before to create a satisfactory system of social justice. By any standard of past experience, the record of recent progress toward human betterment on a world-wide scale has been most impressive. In our time, there has been an awakening of the universal human conscience.

PART TWO: WHAT *SHOULD* BE DONE

Before considering what needs to be done to bring peace to the world, let us briefly review the lessons of history. We have seen from our quickly sketch that it took thousands of years and more, to reach a point of civilization where rules for international conduct were gradually developed and plans were conceived to diminish the incessant warfare that ravaged human life. It was only after the tragedy of World War I that a number of powerful states were prepared to accept proposals for a comprehensive reorganization of international society. The 1919 blueprint for the League of Nations, based upon the evolution and development of ideas put forward over centuries by scholars, statesmen and philosophers, envisaged codification of international law, a court to settle disputes, arms control, collective security and social justice. But sovereign states soon proved unwilling to honor the principles of the Covenant they had accepted. It took the shock of World War II to stimulate a renewal of promises after 1945 that the world would be reorganized to preserve peace. The principles of international criminal law enunciated at Nuremberg were hailed by the world community as a new means to deter aggression and crimes against humanity. The U.N. Charter, although an improvement on the Covenant, still did not go far enough; its effectiveness depended upon the unity of powerful countries with conflicting ideologies. Furthermore, such key Charter mandates as national disarmament and the creation of an international force were never implemented. When fear and suspicion paralyzed reason, confrontation replaced cooperation.

We have sketched some of the progress made in satisfying the prerequisites for a tranquil international order. The clarifications, convention, treaties, consensus definitions and codes have — despite deficiencies — been encouraging. The increased availability of judicial systems to resolve disputes, and the spread of international courts on a regional level are other favorable developments. The expansion of the U.N. to almost universal membership, the creation of many new international institutions to cope with an enormous array of economic and social problems and the birth of such new regional associations as the European Parliament, the Organization of American States and the Organization of African Unity are clear indicators of increased efficiency within the international system.

The Law of the Sea Treaty, governing more than 70% of the planet, holds forth even greater promise. In the area of arms control, the record — though disappointing — has also included the establishment of nuclear-free zones and measures to restrict testing of nuclear weapons, restrain proliferation and curtail certain strategic arms. U.N. Peace-keeping Forces have been effective in many regions. The efforts to bring about a greater degree of social justice have been impressive. The growing awareness and protection of human rights, the abundance of U.N. Specialized Agencies and other international organizations that cope with problems of economic development, health, food, education, housing, environment, and the special needs of women, children, the sick, the aged, and refugees, was unimaginable not many years ago. At the same time, there are worldwide efforts to cope with population increases that influence standards of living and dying throughout the world. It must be borne in mind that the measures we have been considering — laws, courts, and enforcement by improved world organization, disarmament, sanctions and an international army, as well as social justice — can be most effective if, like the fingers of a hand, they all move together in a firm and coordinated way to grasp the vision of peace.

I. Improve International Law

What can we do to move closer toward achieving the first prerequisite, namely the establishment of clearer standards of international behavior? As I indicated at the outset, we all inhabit a planet where many disparate populations have varying and often conflicting values, standards and precepts of moral and legal behavior. There exists no world legislature to decree what each country may or may not do. To a large extent, it is left to nations themselves to decide which customs they will adopt and which versions of ambiguous declarations they will accept as governing their national behavior. Any system that allows competing parties to interpret existing codes solely on the basis of their own advantage is unworthy of respect since it is practically no legal system at all. It is essential that international law be clarified. How should it be done?

A. BALANCE CONFLICTING PRINCIPLES

Several things are needed to obtain greater acceptance of international law. First, there must be a change in attitude. Too often, nations are blinded by their own slogans, and politics displaces principle. There must be greater recognition that all values are relative and cannot be asserted in a vacuum. Freedom of the press, for example — so vital in rich democratic states — has lesser appeal in regions where the primary goal may be to teach an illiterate population how to read. Freedom of speech (the right to shout "Fire!") has its limits in a crowded theater. Just as the right of every individual is necessarily restricted by the rights of others, states should not be allowed to exercise sovereign prerogatives in ways that are detrimental to the international community. National needs must also take account of international needs. There must be greater tolerance and compassion for sincere differences in perspective regarding what is required for the well-being of all peoples. Even the most sacred traditions may be subject to modification to meet changing demands and circumstances. What is needed is a synthesis of different wisdoms as we seek agreement on an acceptable common law of humankind.

International society must balance inconsistent principles if conflict is to be diminished. Self-determination, for example — a principle supported by Article 1(2) of the Charter — is a noble concept that fires many hearts, yet to give it full reign would bring it into conflict with the equally hallowed doctrine protecting territorial integrity of states. Almost all countries have large cultural, religious or ethnic minorities. There are, for example, some thirty-five million Ukrainians, nine million Uzbeks and millions of Lithuanians and Latvians who are now part of the Soviet Union — to say nothing of the Kurds in Iraq, the Welsh in the United Kingdom, the Quebecois in Canada, the Hispanics, Indians and Blacks in the United States, and the millions of persons in India and Africa who have different ethnic loyalties than the dominant national group. If they were all to assert a right to self-determination, no national boundary would be secure and the prevailing anarchy in international affairs would be further aggravated. All minority groups, including those seeking freedom from colonial oppression, must recognize that, although they are entitled to protection of fundamental rights, there are limits to the extent to which they can use violence to determine their own destiny. Proud attachment to ancient traditions and ancestral homelands enriches the spirit of man, but, as the American melting pot and many successful re-settlement programs prove, even displaced peoples can find relative happiness if they are helped to live in conditions of human dignity. This is not to suggest that there can never be changes in the existing territorial entities. Every map-maker knows there is nothing permanent about national boundaries; many a country that fought fiercely for its identity no longer appears on the roster of nations. If the cost of achieving worthwhile goals is too high in terms of overall human suffering as balanced against limited human gain, then some compromise may be required in the general human interest.

Non-interference in the internal affairs of another state is another cherished principle that must be viewed in a broader context. Like self-determination, those who call upon it seldom fail to mention that it is "enshrined" in the U.N. Charter and many other international instruments. In the past, nations did not consider it their legal obligation, or right, either individually or collectively, to intervene when an independent sovereign state committed atrocious acts against its own nationals. Manifestations of concern by way of verbal protests were not uncommon, such as in the case of the Armenian massacres in Turkey in 1915-1916 or the mass killings by the Bolsheviks in Russia in 1918, but such protests were diplomatic and did not involve any overt acts to halt the objectionable conduct. The Nuremberg principles, as unanimously affirmed by the United Nations, made it clear that genocidal mistreatment of a nation's own citizens was a crime against humanity, for which the offenders — including heads of state — could be punished. Humanitarian intervention to halt such illegal acts would presumably be lawful — despite the general rule against non-interference in another nation's internal affairs.

The non-use of force is another hallowed principle that finds support in the U.N. Charter Article 2(4), and other generally accepted international legal instruments going back to the Kellogg-Briand Pact of 1928. Yet, the United States did not hesitate to intervene militarily in several Latin American countries when it was felt that U.S. economic, political or security interests were being jeopardized or U.S. citizens were being threatened. The Soviet Union has taken similar action for similar reasons, in Czechoslovakia, Hungary, Afghanistan and elsewhere. Accepted principles of international law protecting the "territorial integrity" and "political independence" of states, have been brushed aside. An attempt has been made to invest such forceful interventions with an aura of law by characterizing the actions as self-defense or as part of a unilaterally declared self-serving "Doctrine" bearing the name of the particular Decision-Maker in power at the time — ranging from the Monroe Doctrine of 1823 to the Brezhnev Doctrine — more than a century later. Both the United States and the Soviet Union have argued that its use of force was always justified and lawful whereas similar action by the adversary was denounced as illegal and immoral. The need for reconciliation of such conflicting views and principles is obvious — if peace is to be protected.

The matter is even more complicated since the principles of permissible behavior are themselves in a state of constant flux to meet changing social expectations. The general condemnation of genocide, for example, as a crime against humanity because it offends the conscience of mankind may, at some future date, be extended to cover the activities of "death squads" operating under governmental protection. Terrorism is already generally condemned as violative of international law. If a country, or group of countries, decides not to export its oil, that decision is now generally viewed as a purely internal affair and not subject to any interference from abroad. The same may be said of another nation that decides not to export its surplus grains. Yet, if — as a consequence of such internal decisions — millions of innocent people freeze or starve to death, should the international community remain aloof? The general right to life — which is fundamental to all law — may have to be balanced against a state's entitlement to do as it sees fit with vital resources that (due to fortuitous circumstances) happen to be under its national control. New norms are being debated and developed regarding a "New International Economic Order" where two fundamental — and possibly conflicting —principles of contemporary international law, sovereign equality of states and the duty to cooperate, must be balanced. If a state is sovereign and has the right to control its own resources, how can it be made to cooperate by making concessions to the needs of its neighbors? The point is that no rights can be considered to be immutable and absolute; they are subject to change and must be weighed against other rights. If violent conflict is to be averted, one must try to reach some accommodation of competing demands — that is, indeed, the basic goal of the legal process.

B. BRIDGE THE IDEOLOGICAL GAP

Differences between the two superpowers — the United States and the Soviet Union — now pose the greatest threat to world peace. To see what can be done to bridge the ideological gap between these great and powerful nations, one must consider the frictions that continue to rend the fabric of international society. From the American perspective, the incompatibility between communism and capitalism seems irreconcilable. Marxist-Leninist doctrines call for the overthrow of the capitalist class by a revolution and dictatorship of the proletariat. Communist dogma decrees that dissent is to be suppressed; private property is to be seized, and organized religion — the opiate of the masses — is to be discouraged. American history books decry the violent birth of the Soviet system in 1917, together with the brutal slayings of the Russian aristocracy, land-owners and large numbers of innocent people. The current climate of suspicion is intensified by the memory of Stalin's perfidy in signing a pact with Hitler in 1939, of the Russian invasion of Finland, and by the Red Army's post-war refusal to depart from its neighboring states until communist régimes were installed. The Soviet suppression of freedom in Czechoslovakia, Hungary and Poland have not been forgotten. The continuing occupation of Afghanistan by Russian troops remains a sore point. Expansion of Soviet influence throughout the globe and the establishment of socialist governments in parts of Asia, Africa, and particularly in such countries of the western hemisphere as Cuba and Nicaragua, is seen as a threat to the survival of democracy; it contributes to American fears that communist subversion and Soviet aggression must be contained if vital American interests are to be protected and preserved. The growth of Soviet military power increases the appehension. Restrictions on emigration, and other human rights violations add to the litany of complaints that prompted President Ronald Reagan once to refer to the Soviet Union as "the focus of evil in the modern world."

On June 15, 1983, the U.S. Secretary of State, speaking for the President, addressed the Senate Foreign Relations Committee and outlined the Administration's perception of the current Soviet challenge and the American response. Four Soviet activities were described as being unacceptable to the United States: 1 - The Soviet quest for military superiority; 2 - Soviet direct and indirect involvement in unstable areas of the Third World; 3 - Soviet efforts to impose its own ideological model on nominally independent client states; 4 - Moscow's practice of stretching agreements — such as the Helsinki Accords and prohibitions against biological warfare — to the brink of violation and beyond. It was U.S. policy to respond to the perceived challenge by: 1 -Restoring the military balance; 2 - Resisting encroachment on vital interests of the U.S. and its allies; 3 - Supporting those who opposed the Soviet model; 4 - Leaving no doubt about U.S. determination to defend its interests. American strength was to be enhanced by programs to increase the political, military and economic power of the United States and its friends. Containment and détente were no longer considered adequate to counter the world-wide reach of the Soviet state. According to the Secretary, the U.S.S.R. could only be restrained by the West's renewed determination to strengthen its defenses, enhance its political and economic cohesion and oppose Soviet adventurism.

Tensions between the Soviet Union and the United States flared anew when, on September 1, 1983, Soviet military aircraft shot down a Korean passenger plane, killing 269 people. The plane had strayed over Soviet airspace, and there was reason to believe that the pursuit aircraft thought they were firing at an American spy plane that had been in the area. But the American President denounced the Russian action as a "crime against humanity" and "an act of barbarism born of a society which wantonly disregards individual rights and the value of human life and seeks constantly to expand and dominate other nations." A unanimous U.S. Congressional resolution described the event as "one of the most infamous and reprehensible acts in history."

Although the international atmosphere was charged with high tension, when President Reagan appeared to address the U.N. General Assembly later that very month, he declared: "A nuclear war cannot be won and must never be fought." Despite the harsh rhetoric elsewhere, the American President told the assembled world leaders that America was willing to be flexible and to compromise. "The door to an agreement is open," he said. "It is time for the Soviet Union to walk through it." According to the President, America's aims were "to replace a world at war with one where the rule of law would prevail, where human rights were honored, where development would blossom, where conflict would give way to freedom from violence." The head of the U.S. government was, in other words, confirming a commitment to law, social justice and the peaceful settlement of disputes.

To understand the Soviet point of view and the reasons for Russian apprehension and hostility, we must recall that capitalism, as epitomized by the United States, is still seen as a social system for exploiting the working class. The Russians point to American unemployment, inflation, recessions and poverty as indicators that the capitalist system, when compared with the blessings of Soviet socialism, will be "buried" by history. Old Russian leaders remember that American, British, French and Japanese expeditionary forces landed at Murmansk and Archangel in 1918 and 1919 to support an attempted counter-revolution against the Bolsheviks, and that the Soviets were not accorded diplomatic recognition by the United States until 1933. They are not oblivious to the continuing cold-war condemnations and denunciations of Soviet policies and practices. The United States is perceived as an enemy of all socialist countries, and its intervention in the affairs of other nations is seen as an effort to preserve an unjust status quo in order to continue to extract benefits for the rich at the expense of the poor. The use of overt and covert American military might, such as in Korea, Vietnam, Cuba, the Middle East and Latin America, is decried as evidence of America's imperialistic designs. Its economic and military aid to dictatorial and repressive regimes in various parts of the world is condemned as further proof of American malevolence and hypocrisy. The growth of American weaponry, on land, sea and in the air, the deployment of nuclear missiles all around the Soviet Union as well as plans to build an impenetrable shield in space, are viewed as U.S. coercion and preparation for nuclear war.

Soviet Foreign Minister, Andrei Gromyko, a faithful servant of the communist regime for many years, reviewed his nation's foreign policy at a meeting of the Supreme Soviet in Moscow on June 16, 1983. His main complaint was that hostile actions of a political and economic nature were being taken by the "class adversary" against the countries of socialism. He condemned the desire of "the imperialist circles" for military superiority, and insisted that the Soviet Union was entitled to "equality and equal security." When Soviet Ambassador Oleg Troyanovsky, addressed the U.N. General Assembly on October 4 (Gromyko having been denied normal landing rights at New York airports because of the Soviets' downing of the Korean plane), he explained that Soviet policy "aimed at preserving and strengthening peace, promoting détente, curbing the arms race and expanding and deepening cooperation among states." Soviet President Brezhnev had branded the idea of winning a nuclear war as "dangerous madness." Peaceful co-existence, disarmament and international cooperation were the declared goals of the Soviet Union.

None of these stated Soviet objectives seemed to conflict with the aims enunciated by President Reagan, when he addressed the nations of the world. U.S. Secretary of State Shultz had also made plain that "A peaceful world order does not require that we and the Soviet Union agree on all the fundamentals of morals or politics." He did not regard mutual hostility as an immutable fact of international life. The differences between the U.S. and the U.S.S.R. certainly did not seem to be so disparate that either side would be justified in destroying humankind in order to achieve its own particular ends. As former U.S. Ambassador to the Soviet Union, Professor George Kennan of Princeton, put it: "There is no issue at stake in our political relations with the Soviet Union — no hope, no fear, nothing to which we aspire, nothing we would like to avoid — which could conceivably be worth a nuclear war."

If we look beyond the bristling rhetoric (often intended for local political consumption), and see the broader objectives advocated by both Russian and American leaders, the path to a workable accommodation between the Soviet Union and the United States is not impossible to find. What is needed is for the leaders of both nations to muster the will, wisdom, determination, patience and courage to take the necessary specific steps toward the declared common goals.

America has officially stated that it seeks "to engage the Soviet Union in a constructive dialogue . . . to find political solutions to outstanding issues." The Soviet Union has declared that it seeks to find "a common language, and most important of all, common decisions despite all differences of opinion." The Soviet Chairman addressing the Central Committee of the Communist Party, on February 13, 1984, declared his loyalty to "the principle of peaceful coexistence of states with different social systems." He went on to affirm: "We need no military superiority. We do not intend to dictate our will to others . . . We are for a peaceful settlement of all disputable international problems through serious, equal and constructive talks." President Reagan, outlining U.S. policy as one of "credible deterrence, peaceful competition and constructive cooperation, has said: "Conflicts of interest between the Soviet Union and the United States are real, but we can and must keep the peace between our two nations and make it a better and more peaceful world for all mankind." Former President Richard Nixon, in his 1983 book, "Real Peace — A strategy for the West," took a similar view:

> There can be no real peace in the world unless a new relationship is established between the United States and the Soviet Union.
> The two superpowers cannot afford to go to war against each other, at any time or under any circumstances.

Both the United States and the Soviet Union clearly recognize the need for mutual cooperation.

The United States enjoys friendly relations not only with many dictatorial and repressive states, but also with many socialist countries; indeed some of its staunchest allies, such as the Federal Republic of Germany, Israel, England and France, have at various times been under socialist rule. The fact that China has a dedicated communist government does not prevent the United States from seeking good relations with that ancient land. The presence of a militant communist country, Cuba, ninety miles off the U.S. coast, does not noticeably detract from the security or welfare of American citizens. Differences in ideology should not blind nations to the need for all human beings to live together in peace. The leaders of both the Soviet Union and the United States have confirmed that the ideological gap can and must be bridged. The time has come to move beyond the confirmation of general principles — on which essential agreement already exists — and to implement the high-level declarations by specific solutions to the urgent and immediate problems that continue to threaten world peace.

C. ELIMINATE LEGAL LOOPHOLES

Many international agreements, declarations, conventions and other instruments have been accepted by consensus of the world community for the purpose of stipulating or clarifying the permissible bounds of international behavior. Almost all such instruments, including the U.N. Charter, the "Friendly Relations Declaration," the Helsinki Accords, the Manila Declaration of 1982, the consensus definition of aggression and the conventions to outlaw terrorism and crimes against diplomats, contain artfully constructed clauses deliberately formulated with such skillful ambiguity as to allow parties to interpret the vague phrases in ways that further their own national interests. Machiavellian deception, unfortunately, has not yet disappeared from international relations.

For example, the consensus definition of aggression leaves it to the Security Council to decide whether or not aggression has been committed. Those who are most capable of committing aggression are the Permanent Members of the Security Council. Each one has veto power and it should be quite obvious that none of them would be likely to vote to condemn itself. In fact, in the decade since the definition was accepted by consensus, the Security Council — which was to be guided by the definition — has all but ignored it. It is common sense that if nations really wish to curb and condemn aggression as an international crime, any accused party should be excluded from voting on the determination whether or not the offense has been committed.

Many groups and states still insist upon retaining for themselves the freedom to use every conceivable means to attain their own particular goal; they are unwilling to be bound by rules that are considered necessary and desirable by the overwhelming majority of states. For example, on December 28, 1979, one hundred and eighteen nations agreed to an International Convention Against the Taking of Hostages. It was stipulated that any state party apprehending the offender on its territory was obliged "without exception whatsoever" to prosecute the hostage-taker or to extradite him (Article 8). But Article 9 went on to say that there was no obligation to extradite if the requested State had substantial grounds for believing that the offender was wanted for punishment because of his political opinion. Since many, if not most, hostage-takers are motivated by a political objective, Article 9 provided an escape-clause for states to deny extradition in cases where they shared the political goals of the offender. Obviously, the laws of extradition should be tightend to close some of the existing loopholes that enable those who violate the norms of civilized behavior to escape justice. Article 12 provided another legal loophole — the Convention would not apply to persons who were fighting against "colonial domination and alien occupation and against racist régimes in the exercise of their right of self-determination." Thus, Article 12 would offer a valid defense to a particular hostage-taker who could argue that he was fighting for one of the approved causes. Similar problems were encountered — and similar "solutions" were found — when trying to outlaw terrorism, and the seizure of diplomats. Under such circumstances of legal equivocation, it should surprise no one if acts of terrorism and hostage-taking continue — as in fact, they have done. It is common sense that if laws are written with loopholes, lawbreakers will use the loopholes to do as they please.

The search for consensus should not be allowed to paralyze the international community or force it into accepting what appear to be binding obligations but which, on closer scrutiny, are nothing more than legal evasions. Even if it means forefeiting the coveted consensus, let the obstructionists be clearly indentified as outlaws so that they may receive the condemnation or contempt they deserve for refusing to accept a rule of law. This is not to suggest that their justified grievances should be ignored; negotiations should continue to try to find solutions that are acceptable without jeopardizing innocent lives. But a handful of states, or a small group of fanatics — no matter how sincere — should not be permitted to delay humankind's progress toward a more rational and peaceful world order. Those nations, regardless of size, that are willing to move together toward a lawful world by accepting unambiguous restraints on national conduct that threatens the security or well-being of innocent peoples, will become a more powerful voice for reason in a troubled world.

New international instruments — now being debated — offer renewed opportunities to enhance the rule of law on the side of peace. For example, in 1976, the Soviet Union, mindful of the dangers of nuclear war, proposed that all nations sign a treaty outlawing the use of armed force. It received widespread support at the U.N. among Soviet bloc and non-alligned states that traditionally support Soviet initiatives. The United States and several of its allies were skeptical of Soviet sincerity and opposed the treaty as unnecessary and even harmful, since it might obfuscate similar obligations already enunciated in the Charter and other widely accepted international agreements; negotiations are continuing. Instead of rejecting such initiatives because the motives of the sponsors may be suspect, those who yearn for peace should seize the opportunity to negotiate a truly meaningful treaty that will be free of the traditional legal vagaries. The Legal Committee of the U.N. is filled with competent lawyers who are quite capable of drawing legal documents with clear and unambiguous terms. The opportunity to do so should not be cast aside.

In 1977, after aggression had been defined by consensus, several small states requested the U.N. to resume work on a draft Code of Offenses Against the Peace and Security of Mankind. Such an international criminal statute had first been recommended by President Truman in 1946. Those who favored a code argued that deterring international offenses, such as aggression and crimes against humanity, was a better path to world security than a futile arms race. Those who opposed the drafting effort, including the United States, argued that existing statutes were adequate and as long as states were unwilling to accept any enforcement mechanism, there was no need for a code, and it was just a waste of everyone's time to consider it. Underlying the negative attitudes was the suspicion and distrust between the superpowers that enveloped the international scene.

As the subject of a Code of Offenses was debated in the Legal Committee of the United Nations, it became clear that most nations of the world favored such an enactment and that they also wanted it to build on the Nuremberg principles by including the subsequent conventions and declarations that had outlawed terrorism, apartheid and racial discrimination. Many states also wanted new offenses added to the list, such as violations of treaties prohibiting the use of nuclear or biological weapons, pollution of the environment as well as economic crimes. The problem of drafting a new and more comprehensive criminal statute that would seek to define and deter criminal acts by states and their leaders was referred to the International Law Commission — where the matter is now under deliberation. Instead of opposing progress on this difficult issue, all nations should exert their best efforts to clarify the rules of international behavior.

Codification, in addition to contributing to certainty in the law, is — as we have noted a norm-creating process. The international community can ill afford to discard the benefits of deliberation, consultation, negotiation and compromise on difficult issues that threaten the future of mankind — even if some participants are considered insincere, or the burden is time-consuming and onerous. Vituperative rhetoric is never constructive; no nation ever became or remained a world leader merely by saying "No". It is common sense that those who wish to live under the protection of law cannot find protection through the evasion of law. All nations that really long for peace should be eager and willing to accept laws without loopholes.

II. Increase the Judicial Role

Regarding the second prerequisite for a peaceful world — strengthening the judicial process — everything possible should be done to increase the use of mediation or conciliation by third parties or impartial tribunals to settle international disputes that cannot be resolved by negotiation.

A. SETTLE LEGALLY — NOT LETHALLY

Nations must recognize and accept the idea that there are alternate and better ways of settling differences than by the use of destructive force. The reason why the Soviet Union would not accept international adjudication was first made plain by Soviet Ambassador Maxim Litvinoff in 1933, when he addressed the League of Nations Commission that was considering a French peace plan calling for compulsory arbitration, disarmament and an international police force. Litvinoff noted that the U.S.S.R. was the only Socialist country in the world. He pointed to the continuing hostility of capitalist states that had intervened in an attempt to overthrow the 1917 revolution and whose foreign policy was still centered on a crusade against the Soviet Union. "In such circumstances," he said, "it is permissible to enquire whether the Soviet Union may expect a fair attitude towards it and impartial decisions from any international organ." He made it clear that his government did not reject the principle of compulsory adjudication but only that it could not be considered until impartiality and fairness were assured. Another objection that he raised was the absence of a definition of aggression — a shortcoming which would make it impossible for any court to decide which state was the aggressor.

The Soviet reasons for opposing an international court may have been persuasive in 1933; but they are not persuasive half a century later, when the circumstances that may have justified the original intransigence have changed. The Soviet Union can no longer argue that it is the only Socialist state in the world; there are more people living under socialism today than under any other form of government. The decisions of the World Court do not reflect any anti-Soviet bias and the presence of Soviet and Polish judges, as well as many distinguished scholars from non-allligned nations, is an added guarantee of fairness. Furthermore, the Soviet-sponsored definition of aggression has — with modifications — been accepted by consensus. It is time for the Soviet Union to rethink its opposition to an international court and to recognize that circumstances have changed and that its original reasons for opposing such a court have disappeared. The Soviet Union, which lost 20 million of its citizens during World War II, should be able to recognize that the canons of judicial ethics offer a far better safeguard to the Soviet people than the cannons of nuclear war.

It is also high time for the United States to rethink its position regarding the International Court. President Truman, on authorization of the Senate, filed a declaration recognizing the authority of the Court on questions of international law. But (as required by the "Connally Amendment"), it specifically excluded all disputes that the United States might unilaterally declare to be within its own domestic jurisdiction. A nation that gives the appearance of accepting the competence of a court and at the same time denies to the tribunal the normal powers of every judicial agency, or seeks — on technical grounds — to withdraw from the court when it becomes a defendant, undermines both the court and the process of law; it also diminishes respect for itself. The American reservations of 1946, and subsequent challenges to the Court's authority, may be seen as a hypocritical manifestation of scorn for the process of law, on which this great nation was founded. What may have been tolerable in the pre-nuclear past is intolerable now. The fifteen members of the ICJ are all mature men of distinguished legal background; coming from various areas of the world. They are elected to nine-year terms after approval by both the General Assembly and the Security Council. There is no valid reason to doubt their ability to reach wise and fair judgments. It is time for the United States to repeal the Connally Amendment and accept the rule of law — as has long been recommended by the U.S. Department of State and many American experts.

Dr. C. Wilfred Jenks, a very distinguished international legal scholar, wrote an excellent book in 1964 in which he meticulously analyzed *The Prospects of International Adjudication*. Based on thirty-five years of study, he concluded:

All of which we cherish most in our existing heritage of law

and freedom is due to the visionaries of long ago . . . No free
society has ever endured, or can endure, except on the basis
of the rule of law. . . We are in the earliest stages of groping
toward a world order based on a common law of mankind in
which international adjudication takes its place with
international legislation and international administration
among the instruments of peace, order and good government
on a world basis.

As more states increasingly participate in international adjudication of
disputes, the effectiveness of the decisions is enhanced, for they
command growing respect and loyalty from those nations that have
joined together to settle their differences by judicial-type proceedings
rather than by the traditional alternative means — the use of force. The
lesson that is being learned is that sovereign states can derive mutual
benefits from yielding part of their sovereignty to an objective tribunal
with authority to resolve differences in a peaceful and binding way. It is
only common sense that in a nuclear age it is far better to settle
problems legally rather than lethally.

B. INTERNATIONAL COURTS FOR INTERNATIONAL CRIMES

Both the United States and the Soviet Union — as well as others
—should alter their current opposition to an international criminal
court. Both nations acted as partners when the International Military
Tribunal at Nuremberg gave new hope to the world that those
responsible for aggression, genocide and crimes against humanity would
not escape justice. As had been noted, those who supported the creation
of the IMT believed they were building a law for the future. The many
arguments that have been made to support the creation of an
international criminal court as part of the arsenal of humankind against
the continuation of international crimes has been meticulously described
elswhere (See B.B. Ferencz, *An International Criminal Court)* and need
not be repeated here. The conviction that law, courts and punishment
serve to deter crimes — a premise that is accepted by all law-abiding
states — should also be persuasive regarding international crimes; even
if it is more difficult to apprehend the offenders.

The Soviet Union has opposed the creation of any permanent
international criminal jurisdiction as a usurpation of Soviet sovereignty.
Since the United States was the principal advocate of the international
criminal court at Nuremberg — as well as the subsequent war crimes
tribunals — its opposition to an international criminal jurisdiction has
been less articulated but no less determined. In a 1981 article, V. P.
Shupilov of the Institute of Crime Prevention in Moscow, suggested
that once cooperation and peaceful coexistence between the two
competing social systems became a reality, it might be possible for the
Soviets to accept some limitation of their national sovereignty to the
extent of accepting a system that would make international criminal law
and the Nuremberg principles enforceable — another illustration of the

importance of linkage. If the Soviets show some inclination to accept an international penal court, the United States should be true to the high ideals that prompted its creation of the first international criminal court in the past, and join in creating such a tribunal. Detailed plans for an international criminal court have been prepared and could quickly be implemented.

The need for an international penal court did not end with World War II. Since that time, many deeds not previously characterized as international crimes have been generally outlawed by widely accepted international conventions. Among such offenses may be mentioned genocide, apartheid, terrorism, killing diplomats, taking hostages, hijacking aircraft, torture, the use of mercenaries, slavery and similar acts that outrage and jeopardize people everywhere. Most such offenses could hardly take place without the complicity or connivance of a national government. The same is true for many political assassinations, the "disappearance" of thousands of innocent citizens or their murder by "death squads" that evade apprehension. National governments that are themselves accomplices can hardly be relied upon to enforce international laws that would condemn them. Is it not common sense that if such heinous acts are universally condemned as international crimes, there should be an international court to deal with them?

In 1950, after years of study, a panel of the International Law Commission, led by Ricardo Alfaro, former President of Panama, recommended that an international criminal court should be created as an independent agency or as a chamber of the ICJ. Alfaro, who later became Vice-President of the World Court, wrote: "If the rule of law is to govern the community of states and protect it against violations of the international public order, it can only be satisfactorily established by the promulgation of an international penal code and by the permanent functioning of an international criminal jurisdiction." It is time for the advice of this distinguished and impartial jurist to be accepted by the international community.

Professor Robert A. Friedlander, an outstanding authority on ways to curb terrorism, recently wrote:

> Let the nations of the world promulgate precise, definite, binding statutes which would identify and penalize terrorist activities of whatever type, and would make extradition compulsory if the host country refused to try the expatriate offender. Alternative jurisdiction should be given to an International Criminal Court. . . A truly international court with compulsory jurisdictin over international crimes could become a global symbol for the rule of law.

There is no good reason for nations and their bureaucrats to remain frozen into the positions and attitudes of the past. Consideration has been given to establishing an international criminal chamber as part of the present World Court. But that was ruled out as too cumbersome since it would require an amendment of the Court's statute. Perhaps thought should be given to enabling the existing Courts of Human Rights to cope with allegations of human rights abuses that have reached the level of international crimes. The fact that it was never done before is hardly a persuasive reason to reject any innovation.

C. HONOR THE CHARTER OBLIGATIONS

When we speak of enhancing the judicial role or of strengthening the judicial process, it is not meant in the narrow sense of using only an established court or tribunal. Many disputes that may lead to war are not legal in nature and are not particularly amenable to strictly legal determination. Such controversies can be dealt with in other judicial-type proceedings. Many nations, such as China and several African countries, have traditions that do not favor recourse to third parties to settle disputes. In such instances, there remains available the traditional methods of direct negotiation or diplomacy to reach a peaceful settlement. The U.N. Charter directs parties first to seek a solution by "negotiation, enquiry, mediation, conciliation, arbitration, judicial settlement, resort to regional agencies or arrangements or other peaceful means of their own choice." There is thus a wide array of options, most of which have been developed over the years and which are now governed by agreed rules or conventions. Any one or more of these peaceful methods for resolving disputes is perfectly acceptable.

The existence and growth of regional agencies authorized to render binding judgments regarding human rights violations or breaches of economic treaties is an encouraging trend that must be further expanded. The Law of the Sea dispute-setlement machinery — that has been widely accepted — offers an outstanding new model for the resolution of conflicts that might otherwise pose a threat to peace. All treaties should encompass provisions for the peaceful resolution of differences of interpretation. As international society continues to expand and to be governed by a plethora of international administrative agencies dealing with technical and specialized multinational problems, they must continue to create their own tribunals to resolve disputes that might give rise to friction among nations.

International institutions of many kinds can play an ever-increasing role in adjusting conflicts between competing groups or nations. The procedures for fair determination of complicated international issues are being increasingly developed and these should be coordinated and consolidated into general rules that will be seen to be just and will therefore find broad acceptance. The right to appear before international tribunals of various kinds should be expanded so that organizations having legitimate interests, as well as individuals whose rights are violated within their own country, may find a forum in which important grievances that affect persons everywhere can be aired and adjudicated. The very least that should be done is to encourage existing tribunals of all kinds to issue advisory opinions on serious issues that might affect the peace of a community. All of these techniques for peaceful settlement would be consistent with the mandates of the U.N. Charter.

What should not be acceptable to the world community is the threat or use of armed force in any manner inconsistent with the Charter. According to Article 51, force is only permissible if used in self-defense against an armed attack — and only until the Security Council can restore peace. It is both barbaric and illegal for national leaders to send their youth out to be killed or to kill for reasons that have never been sanctioned by the world body. Since wars of any size always harbor the dangerous risk that they may escalate to nuclear annihilation, the hazard of even limited or localized violence is too great to be tolerated by the rest of society. It is only common sense that all nations should be required to honor their obligations under a Charter they have pledged to respect. But how to enforce that obligation is the problem.

III. Enforce International Law

Enforcement of law — the third essential requirement for any legal system — is the most difficult to achieve. Its success, as we have noted, depends upon an improved international order, arms control, effective sanctions, an international military force and social justice.

A. REFORM THE UNITED NATIONS

It has already been mentioned that visions of an improved world order were conceived by many philosophers and thinkers. Many scholars were quick to point out that the present Charter of the United Nations required revision. The outstanding seminal work by Grenville Clark and Professor Louis B. Sohn of Harvard called for "world-scale institutions corresponding to those which have been found essential for the maintenance of law and order in local communities and nations." Private individuals and organizations have joined in the demand that the U.N. Charter be modified to make it more effective. For over a decade, forty-seven nations have met regularly as a Special Committee on the Charter of the United Nations and on Strengthening the Role of the Organization. There has thus been widespread recognition of the need for Charter reform and no shortage of talent directed toward making the United Nations a more useful instrumentality for the enforcement of world peace.

The most glaring deficiency of the U.N. system is its voting procedures. A General Assembly, which allows one vote to each nation, regardless of territorial size, strength, population, literacy or contribution to the organization, is manifestly undemocratic, unfair and unrealistic. Proposals for an improved voting structure based upon various forms of proportional representation have come from many sources. Clark and Sohn suggested a system based upon a minimum of one vote for every nation, no matter how small, but a maximum of thirty for such populous nations as China, India, the U.S. and the U.S.S.R. The

Campaign for U.N. Reform — a private American organization — has urged that tiny nations, such as the Seychelles with a population of only 67,000, be given "associate state" status, with limited financial burdens and limited voting privileges. The World Association of World Federalists has suggested a bicameral General Assembly to include an elected "House of Peoples." The Center for War/Peace Studies, has developed an interesting "Binding Triad" proposal: Assembly resolutions would require two-thirds majority votes based upon membership, population and wealth and if all three tests are met, then the resolutions would become binding law.

Harold Stassen, a frequent candidate for the Presidency of the United States and a former Governor of the State of Minnesota — who helped draft, and signed, the original Charter of the U.N. in 1945 — has proposed a revised Charter which includes a Central Cabinet of twenty-two Administrators and a system of weighted voting that would range from one vote for the smallest state to 1000 votes for the ten major states. The standing of states would take into account their populations, annual gross national product, and per capita production. The Cabinet would have primary authority regarding the oceans and space and could make recommendations on other matters. It would thus be a representative supplement to the other existing agencies. From the many suggestions that have been made for a revision of the existing voting procedures of the General Assembly, it is clear that some improvement along the lines of a more democratic and equitable representation is essential if the Assembly is to play a more constructive role in the search for world peace.

Carlos P. Romulo of the Phillipines, who also helped to draft the original U.N. Charter, when interviewed in 1984, at the age of 85, said that the U.N. would have to be reformed or it would collapse into total irrelevance and nuclear war would follow. He called for a standing U.N. army, relinquishment of the veto power in the Security Council and an obligation for all warring nations to settle by binding arbitration.

As has already been noted, the existence of the veto power on the part of each Permanent Member of the Security Council meant that the enforcement arm of the United Nations could only function if there were unanimity among its most powerful members. This fatal flaw has remained uncorrected simply because those with the power of final decision were not prepared to relinquish it — even if it meant undermining the effectiveness of the organization on which other nations and all peoples had pinned their hopes for world security. Small and weak states pose no threat to anyone and they are as concerned as others — if not more so — regarding the safety of their society. The powerful states granted to themselves the monopoly of power in the U.N. — there is no valid reason why that should remain immutable. There should be an expansion of the membership of the Security Council to make it more representative of the world as it is today, rather than what it was in 1945. The number of votes needed to pass a Security Council resolution can be increased to two-thirds, or even more, if all states are to be bound by the final decision. But it takes only common sense to see that a security organization that can only function with the consent of those who are most likely to jeopardize world security is more a formula for insecurity than world tranquility.

The Charter did not foresee the important role that would be played by militant non-governmental groups, religious associations or political parties with a capacity to disrupt the social order. The reach of the Secretary-General should not be restricted solely to considering or investigating disputes between nation-states. Furthermore, there is need to improve U.N. procedures for ascertaining the facts and issues in any potential or actual conflict. Since the Security Council often uses its power to stop or delay investigations that might not serve the interests of one of the Permanent Members, what is required to avoid such abuse is the appointment of an impartial investigative commission that would be available on a permanent basis with authority to investigate and report the truth regarding any conflict anywhere in the world. It is common sense that a local fire inspector who is always available and responsible for reporting as soon as there is smoke in the area can be much more effective than a distant *ad hoc* brigade that must be newly assembled every time one of the neighbors may choose to sound an alarm. Public investigative and fact-finding commissions composed of reliable and reputable observers would strengthen the effectiveness of diplomacy and other forms of peaceful intervention; and would help to mobilize public opinion on the side of justice and peace. The Special Committee dealing with Charter Reform is already considering proposals for the establishment of a permanent commission of good offices, mediation and conciliation for the settlement of disputes. Preventing a conflict may be easier than halting one and the use of United Nations machinery should be a first resort to prevent conflict rather than a last resort.

There is no doubt that the administration of the United Nations is so wasteful and inefficient that it seriously hampers the ability of the organization to fulfill its many important functions. Very many of the U.N. staff members and delegates are dedicated, hard-working and intelligent people who are thoroughly devoted to the ideals of a more just and tranquil international society. Yet, they do not all meet those high standards. The Secretariat, which was intended to be an independent international civil service, has in part, turned into a haven for redundant national bureaucrats. Mountains of useless papers — in five languages — and a plethora of committees dealing with related subjects in an uncoordinated way (and often for purely propagandistic purposes) are as costly as they are counter-productive. The Secretary-General, who should be the Chief Administrative Officer with responsibility and authority to direct an efficient worldwide agency, has his hands tied by a General Assembly dominated by small nations that mandate costly and ineffective programs and practices with little consideration for those who must foot the bill. If the U.N. is to regain some of the prestige it enjoyed when it was founded, there is urgent need for change.

As long as the United Nations is unable to reform itself, those nations that are determined to improve the prevailing system must increase their areas of mutual cooperation. New regional alliances for peaceful purposes, increased collaboration between existing blocs of states, exchanges of information and expanded economic cooperation are some of the means that must be pursued if the goal of an improved structure of international society is eventually to be attained. Of all the vital matters that should be attended to, the need for nuclear arms control is by far the most pressing and important. A nuclear time-bomb is ticking and if it is not defused, all other efforts to improve the structure of international society will be futile — there will be no world left to save.

B. CONTROL NATIONAL ARMS

President Dwight D. Eisenhower, in a personal and confidential letter dated April 4, 1965, wrote:

> When we get to the point, as one day we will, that both sides know that in any outbreak of general hostilities, regardless of the element of surprise, destruction will be both reciprocal and complete, possibly we will have sense enough to meet at the conference table with the understanding that the era of armaments has ended and the human race must conform its actions to this truth or die.

The era of armaments should be brought to an end. Before we consider what specific steps can be taken to end the era of armaments, it may be helpful to consider some related factual and theoretical problems that must be faced.

In 1978, a General Assembly Session on Disarmament concluded: "Nuclear weapons pose the greatest danger to mankind and the survival of civilization." An expert U.N. Commission, headed by Anders I. Thunberg of Sweden, concluded in 1980: "A total nuclear war is the highest level of human madness." Jonathan Schell, in his graphic portrayal, *The Fate of the Earth,* has argued convincingly that nuclear warfare means the extinction of mankind forever, and he calls upon this generation and all people to avoid the destruction of the future.

The exact number of existing nuclear weapons is a closely guarded military secret. But it is known without doubt that the number of nuclear warheads possessed by the United States and the Soviet Union exceeds 50,000 and that only a small fraction of that arsenal would suffice to kill every man, woman and child on earth. One American submarine alone could unleash more explosive force than all of the munitions used in World War II. The combined destructive capability of the superpowers exceeds a million Hiroshima bombs. Seventy scientists, including five Nobel-Prize winners, who had worked on the first atomic bomb, testified in April 1983, that the superpowers had the ability to "destroy each other and a significant part of the rest of the world many times over."

The technology for achieving such macabre results is very complicated. The instruments for delivering massive devastation by land, sea and air have various reaches, speeds, accuracy and power. They range from tactical nuclear weapons for use on the field of combat to "strategic weapons" launched from a distant haven. There are also plans for particle and laser beams to serve as "killer satellites" in potential future "Star Wars." The systems keep changing to keep pace with new scientific discoveries. The enormous array of sophisticated weaponry, as well as variations in type and quality, makes it possible for each side to argue — through conviction or caution — that the other is ahead. One should not discount the influence of "hawks" — on both sides — or the self-serving persuasions of "the military-industrial complex." Despite difficulties of quantifying the defensive requirements of superpowers and their allies, independent experts, including Nobel-Prize winner Alfonso Garcia Robles of Mexico, were convinced in 1982 that there was essential parity between the ideological adversaries. Neither the Soviet Union nor the United States was prepared to acknowledge that their existing arsenals were adequate. President Reagan, on first coming into office, was committed to closing "the window of vulnerability." The Soviets were determined to match the Americans, step by step. Military leaders in both the Pentagon and the Kremlin were resolved to win the arms race — even if it led to Armageddon.

The language of annihilation speaks in an idiom of its own that is all but incomprehensible to ordinary citizens. Being unable to grasp the intricacies of a wide array of mysterious acronyms, the public is deprived of the capacity to communicate regarding its own destiny and is encouraged to leave matters to military experts. People read of ICBM's (inter-continental ballistic missiles) that are mobile or stationary in silos hard or soft, and MIRV's (multiple independently targetable re-entry vehicles), of ASBM's (air to surface ballistic missiles) — like the "Minuteman III" with a CEP (circular error probable) better than 300 m. (meters) — of SRBM's (short-range ballistic missiles) —like the "Pershing" and "Cruise Missiles" that can hug the earth and destroy Soviet targets within minutes — deployed to offset the threat of Soviet SS-20's aimed at cities of Western Europe. They hear of warheads and launchers — like the B-1 bomber or the Soviet's TU-22M known as "Backfire" — and of submarines named "Poseidon" or "Trident" that can hide beneath the sea until needed to annihilate nations. They learn of megatons and kilotons, and of neutron bombs with a destructive capacity that boggles the mind. When translated into human terms — which is almost never done — the complicated terminology spells death to incredible numbers of men, women and children. Those who think they can live with a nuclear arms race may have a short life-expectancy.

Disarmament negotiations between the United States and the Soviet Union have been going on for many years. There are Strategic Arms Reductions Talks (START), discussions regarding Mutual Balanced Force Reduction (MBFR), negotiations regarding Intermediate Range Nuclear Weapons (INF), and conferences aimed at curbing chemical and bacteriological means of destruction. The negotiators, directed by Decision-Makers in their respective capitols, quibble about the relative numbers of particular weapons, with each side pointing to those where the opponent has a numerical advantage, while minimizing other weapons where the situation is reversed. Each side makes offers that it should know will be unacceptable to the adversary. Mutual fear and suspicion hinders any significant progress. Each superpower warns that without disarmament, the world faces extinction; neither side mentions that the danger is created by the superpowers themselves.

The justification offered for the enormous expenditures on arms of every kind — by both superpowers — is that only through the availability of overwhelming military might can the enemy be deterrred from acts of aggression. It is argued that nuclear weapons are not intended to be used — their purpose is merely a deterrent one to prevent the adversary from using force to achieve an objective that may threaten the other's vital interests. The heart of the theory is that a nation can be induced to forego planned behavior because of the fear that the injury it will sustain in retaliation will be vastly greater than any benefit it might derive from its aggression. Both the Soviet Union and the United States have accepted the deterrence concept as the principal *raison d'être* for their nuclear arsenals. That conclusion is clear from the Anti-Ballistic Missile (ABM) Treaty that was signed by both nations in Moscow on May 26, 1972, and reaffirmed in a 1974 Protocol. Declaring their intention "to achieve at the earliest possible date the cessation of the nuclear arms race and to take effective measures toward reductions in strategic arms, nuclear disarmament, and *general and complete disarmament*" "(underlining added), both parties agreed to deploy ABM systems for the defense of their territory. They thus accepted the proposition that, until effective controls could be worked out, peace could be maintained by mutual assured destruction in the event of war — a theory that bore the appropriate acronym "MAD."

The MAD theory, based on a balance of terror, assumes that man's behavior is governed solely by reason — a highly dubious assumption considering the present state of the world. It is argued that for forty years or more, deterrence has prevented war between the superpowers. Many other factors besides reason determine human behavior. In matters of war and peace, nations are seldom ruled by logic. Irrational "small" wars based on religion or dogma can escalate to nuclear holocaust. Missiles can be launched by accident, by computer error, or by the fury of an uncontrollable fanatic. The dynamics of conflict, like the spiral of arms escalation, acquires a force of its own. The spread of nuclear weapons — despite agreements for non-proliferation — and the possibility of buying, stealing or constructing them, is a temptation that may prove irresistable to groups or nations that are less than reasonable.

The notion of nuclear deterrence is not far removed from the doctrine — discredited by history — that peace can be preserved by a balance of power. That theory may have seemed rational at Westphalia in 1648, when a nation which tipped the military balance in its own favor might expect to emerge the winner; but in a nuclear war, everyone loses and loses everything. As long as scientific technology keeps altering the ratios of nuclear power, each of the rivals must, at one time or another, face the prospect of falling into a vulnerable position. Apprehension is intensified by the secrecy and deception that surrounds everything related to military might. The nation that perceives itself in jeopardy feels compelled to accelerate the arms race; while the nation that considers itself ahead may be tempted to try a pre-emptive first-strike in order to capitalize on its temporary advantage. The oscillating escalation of nuclear weaponry does not enhance international security — it jeopardizes it. It is sheer folly to try to protect the world by threatening to destroy it. The threat is either incredible — in which case it is useless — or it is real — in which case it is too hazardous to be tolerable.

The fundamental idea underlying the theory of nuclear deterrence is that the citizens of target countries will be killed if their nation does not conform to the will of the attacking state. The populations of both superpowers are, in effect, held as mutual hostages under threat of imminent extinction by blast, fire and flame, or lingering death by radiation. The Nuremberg principles, formulated and implemented by the United States and the Soviet Union, and unanimously endorsed by the General Assembly of the United Nations, decreed that any attempt or threat to kill large masses of innocent people was a crime against humanity. Nuclear bombs can make no distinction between soldiers and helpless children; their blast, radiation and fall-out threatens all mankind. The Nuremberg Tribunals held that those persons who were responsible for aggression and crimes against humanity — and only those persons — regardless of rank or station — would be held to criminal account. Yet, if some misguided person in Washington, or Moscow, were to initiate a nuclear attack, the assault — and the predictable nuclear response — would destroy millions of human beings who were in no way at fault. Indeed, among the victims there would certainly be many who (openly or clandestinely) opposed the aggressive policies of their government. The Soviet Union and the United States should be expected to honor the legal and moral precedents they established at Nuremberg, and not retreat to a new order of inhumanity. Human survival should not be made dependent upon the threat of human destruction. It is common sense that world security should not be based upon a theory that is both genocidal and suicidal.

The possession of nuclear weapons by the United States and the Soviet Union, as well as by France, England and China, and the possibility that other countries such as Israel, India, Pakistan, and

South Africa can produce such devices on short notice, makes the need for world-wide nuclear arms limitations ever more urgent. If the superpowers that control the overwhelming share of nuclear force can reach agreement on systematic reductions, it may be expected that other nuclear powers will not stand in the way and will cooperate in the move toward a safer world.

As long as nuclear weapons exist, the expansion of nuclear-free zones can help to diminish the risks and devastation of potential nuclear warfare. We have already mentioned several parts of the world (Antarctica, Latin America, outer space and the sea-bed) that are already protected by verifiable agreements to keep them immune from any type of nuclear hostility. Similar protection is being proposed and should be granted to other regions, such as India, the Middle-East, and the continent of Europe. Non-nuclear states should be given international guarantees that they will be protected if they pledge never to produce nuclear weapons. Nuclear-free zones must be expanded until they cover not merely space and seas and parts of land, but all of Planet Earth. Using weapons of mass destruction as a remedy for ailments in the international order may prove more fatal than the disease. It is only common sense tht it is far better for the human race to end the arms race than for the arms race to end the human race.

C. MAKE SANCTIONS EFFECTIVE: CREATE AN INTERNATIONAL FORCE

The failure of nations to accept a system of effective economic sanctions or to create an international military force, was not a failure of the system, but a failure on the part of those who were entrusted to carry it out. We have seen that after World War I, members of the League of Nations covenanted to enforce international law by diplomatic and economic sanctions. The problems of coordination were thoroughly explored by a large number of technical committees working over a long period of time. They learned what was required to make such a system effective: coordination of action on an international scale, and measures to ameliorate inequitable hardships that might fall upon some of the cooperative states. But the system was never tried. Today, there is a greatly enhanced capacity to inventory the vital resources of the world. Satellites and computers have already accumulated much of the necessary information. Regional economic associations are in a much better position to provide the international cooperation required to make sanctions truly effective. What is required now — as it was then — is for states to honor the committments they voluntarily undertook — both in the Covenant and the Charter. With computerized and comprehensive planning, it should be possible to organize a system of collective economic sanctions that can be activated when required to maintain peace. Those who continue to cling to the status quo and hide behind the old argument: "The time is not yet ripe" should answer the question: "If not now, when?"

The techniques for making peaceful sanctions effective against actions that disrupt world order, are well known; what is lacking is the determination to do what is necessary to achieve the stated goal. For example: In 1977, a Lufthansa plane of the Federal Republic of Germany was hijacked and the passengers held hostage in Yemen until they were freed by a raid of West German commandos. Subsequently, 56,000 pilots in 65 countries threatened to go on strike unless effective action was taken immediately by the United Nations to prevent the recurrence of such crimes. Forty-two countries placed "The Safety of International Civil Aviation" on the U.N. agenda. In July, 1978, the leaders of the United States, Canada, France, the Federal Republic of Germany, Italy, Japan and the United Kingdom — the major aviation powers of the free-world — expressing their common concern about terrorism and the taking of hostages, jointly declared that they would act cooperatively and intensify their efforts to combat international terrorism. They specifically resolved in a public declaration that where a country refused to extradite or prosecute hijackers, they would all "take immediate action to cease all flights to that country." A number of other governments announced similar unilateral committments. Yet, there was no strike and flights were not halted. The governments that had proclaimed their intent to put a stop to aerial piracy were heavily dependent upon oil from Arab states that supported the hijackers. It was politically and economically inexpedient to implement the declared plan to enforce international law. What they should have done is obvious: they should have lived up to their word.

Consider what the impact would be if effective sanctions were imposed to halt the fighting that now takes place in various parts of the world. In the Middle East, for example, if the major arms suppliers to the belligerents were to halt all arms shipments into the area, would not the level of killing at least be reduced, if not eliminated? Would not South Africa have to accelerate its movement away from apartheid if other nations really imposed a total boycott on goods going into or out of that country? Would not Iran and Iraq both have to accept a cease-fire if no nation would import oil from warring states, or lend economic or military aid to any country that continues its military combat? If all exporters of grain were to halt their shipments to the U.S.S.R. until Soviet troops were withdrawn from Afghanistan, how long would it take before the Soviets would rethink their present defiance of the international community? The shipment of weapons to those who make revolution invariably increases the loss of life among those on whose behalf the violence is purportedly being applied. Bullets are no substitute for bread, and deadly explosives cannot fight drought, recession or famine. The imposition of effective economic and diplomatic sanctions is a non-violent way to enforce the universal aspiration for a tranquil world. It is time for the Decision-Makers to listen to the cries of the people.

Whatever measures (economic or military) are applied to constrain the use of force, the humanitarian precept of proportionality should be respected. No more force, or other means of coercion, should be used than is required to attain the lawful objective. "Unconventional warfare" — the term frequently used to describe what others call "terrorism" — can hardly be curbed by a massive military counter-assault that usually engulfs many innocent victims in its wake. Severing sources of supplies and weapons may prove to be more effective in the long run — particularly if they are coupled with sincere efforts to seek accomodation and reconciliation.

If peaceful sanctions prove inadequate, then, as a last resort, nations must turn to the international military force that was foreseen and promised by both the Covenant of the League of Nations and the U.N. Charter. Article 43, specifically provides that members will "make available to the Security Council, on its call and in accordance with a special agreement or agreements, armed forces, assistance and facilities. . . " A Military Staff Committee, representing the Chiefs of Staff of the five Permanent Members, is to assist the Council in maintaining peace. As has been noted, by 1947, a detailed plan for the creation of the international forcce was worked out and consensus was reached on the most important principles. But very soon thereafter, further progress came to an end. The agreement mandated by the Charter was never reached and the vital enforcement arm of the Security Council was never created. The implied promise of those nations that drafted and signed the Charter was never kept.

Harry Truman was President of the United States when the "cold war" put an end to American and Soviet cooperation. He was the one who unleashed the atomic bomb, inaugurated the United Nations, blocked Soviet expansion in Greece and Turkey, broke the Soviet blockade of Berlin, created NATO and ordered U.S. troops into Korea. After he left office and was in retirement, Truman, writing about the requirements for world peace, noted:

> The leader of one of the great nations whose voice can be heard and listened to should go to the Assembly of the United Nations, and advocate an international control of nuclear energy in the interest of all mankind. He should advocate an international police force for the enforcement of control and the maintenance of peace in the Near East, the Far East, the Pacific, the Atlantic, and all around the world.

In calling for an international army, Truman was echoing ideas that had been espoused by the amphictyonic councils of ancient Greece, by the French after World War I, by Winston Churchill and other world leaders and that had, in fact, been clearly envisaged by the United Nations Charter. That an international military force can be created and that it can be operated effectively, has already been demonstrated by the workings of the embryo U.N. Peacekeeping Forces in many parts of the globe. It is not unreasonable to insist that those who hold high office should make greater efforts to honor the spirit of the pledges made to the peoples of the world.

A properly equipped U.N. force, drawn from non-aligned nations or small states that have no major stake in the particular conflict, would be the most appropriate instrument for disarming belligerents and maintaining peace. What terrorist band or group of insurgents, mercenaries or religious fanatics could long stand up to a U.N. Force —of say a quarter of a million men — assigned to prevent the use of armed violence as a means of settling differences? The time has come for all those who believe in a peaceful world to insist that the Charter plan —even on an *ad hoc* basis — be honored and tried in order to restore normalcy to the lives of those who are engaged in mortal combat. Failure of U.N. members to cooperate in measures of collective security will be a clear indicator that the recalcitrant nation prefers to play power politics with the lives of large numbers of human beings. As long as Permanent Members of the Security Council are unwilling to exercise their enforcement responsibilities under the Charter, many wars will have to be fought until one side collapses in exhaustion or the combatants themselves recognize that the cost in human despair demands that some compromise be reached. A system of sanctions under effective international controls, backed by an international peace force — controlled by the world community rather than big Powers that have failed to discharge their obligations or live up to their word — is what is needed as an essential component of the effort to enforce international law and maintain peace.

D. INCREASE SHARING AND CARING

As has been pointed out, there can be no peace without social justice and no social justice without peace. It is not enough to settle disputes after they have arisen. If we are to expect voluntary compliance with international law, we must seek to eliminate in advance the injustices — real or perceived — that lead to conflict. We have noted some of the significant progress made in recent years to enhance social justice throughout the world. Obviously, even major social engineering efforts are likely to remain inadequate until population growth is brought under better control, or there is some drastically new approach to planetary well-being. The time is rapidly approaching when humankind must regard all of the earth's treasures as a common heritage to be shared on an international and equitable basis. Regional economic unions have already accepted the principle that resources must be allocated in a systematic way that takes account of varied human needs and disparate contributions. Socialist countries have worked with integrated economies for many years, and even every "free society" or capitalist state has imposed controls and taxes designed to bring about a sharing of wealth between "haves" and "have-nots." A system of completely free enterprise no longer exists anywhere on earth. All governments recognize the need for regulations to maintain social equilibriums; it is essentially a matter of degree. The existence of extensive loans from rich nations to poorer nations — loans that may never be repaid — is another manifestation of the same trend. The universal movement toward greater concern for the welfare of human beings everywhere should be encouraged.

Very many lands on all continents offer examples of persecution against innocent persons who do not share the religion, race, color or political convictions of those in power. Unfortunately, those who are not themselves the direct targets of such abuses have too often been willing to shut their eyes to cruelty if it could be rationalized as being in the interest of the state or a popular cause. Too many people are too tolerant of intolerance. When the misuse of others is ignored or accepted, it threatens us all. If we are to live in peace, we must recognize that all persons are entitled to equal opportunity and respect; all of us are our "brother's keeper." Let humans be human.

Oppression can take many forms. Whether a violation of individual liberty comes from the Right or the Left makes very little difference to the victim who is caught in the middle. Those who are denied spiritual sustenance are divested of a vital right. Those who cannot build their own social or cultural institutions, or cherish their ethnic traditions are robbed of their inheritance. Those who are condemned to poverty because their country's exports are needed to pay the interest due on foreign loans are also deprived. There is nothing more poignant than the sight of an emaciated mother seeking food for her starving infant, or children fleeing in terror from the ruins of a home that has just been destroyed by "freedom fighters." To the father who must flee from his country to find support for his family, it makes little difference if he is restrained by a wall keeping him in, or by frontier guards keeping him out. Until national leaders are willing to accept common responsibility for ameliorating economic and social privation — wherever it occurs —no border will be secure. Selfishness will never defeat a demand for social justice. Political independence without economic independence must breed discontent. It is common sense that clamping down a lid of oppression cannot ease tensions, but only increase them, and magnify the dangers of explosion.

It is not a matter of North-South dialogue, or South-South dialogue, or East-West confrontation. The Third World is part of one world. Decision-Makers must move away from parochial perceptions and accept the fact that if we are to dwell together in relative peace on this interdependent planet, all of humankind must be brought under the protective shield of an enlightened international community perpared to shoulder the obligations of caring and sharing in a spirit of universal brotherhood.

In the final analysis, eliminating justified discontent is a matter of self-interest and self-defense. The strength of a nation does not depend solely upon its capacity to destroy other nations and kill its citizens. National security is dependent upon the spirit of its people, their respect for the integrity and decency of its leaders, and their feeling of well-being, and confidence in the justice of their government. An exploitive community without moral fiber will lack cohesion and lose power — despite the vastness of its military arsenal. As long as significant portions of the population feel that they are being used as pawns in an uncertain political struggle — even if they are told that it is for their own good or to fulfill some historical destiny — the lack of confidence will encourage young people into activities and attitudes that will sap the stamina, determination and unity of the country. By contrast, a government that by its deeds has earned the friendship and admiration of people everywhere need have no fear for the security of its citizens.

PART THREE: WHAT *CAN* BE DONE

I. Settle by Compromise

According to the ancient adage: "Where there is a will, there is a way." But the central and unresolved problem still remains — what can realistically be done to generate the will that is needed by Decision-Makers in order to halt existing conflicts and to accept the changes required for a more rational world order? We have seen that after the horrors of each world war, nations recognized — at least for a fleeting moment — that change was necessary; but the small steps taken in new directions were halting and inadequate. It was not that those in authority did not know what was required to establish a system of enforceable international law — that had been carefully laid out in detailed plans by competent and dedicated scholars; the political leaders simply did not dare enough or did not care enough. After the first nuclear explosion, Albert Einstein noted: "The unleashed power of the atom has changed everything save our modes of thinking, and we thus drift toward unparalleled catastrophes." It is common sense to recognize that, faced with the possibility of nuclear annihilation, it is far better for nations not to test their survivability but to make needed changes *before* war occurs. Yet, many political leaders still prefer to mislead rather than to lead. If those in high office are unwilling or unable to act in the interests of the humankind they profess to benefit, it is also common sense that they should be replaced. A handful of men of narrow vision can not usurp the authority to decide the fate of the world. The earth may have begun with a big bang, but no one vested a few mortals with the right to decide that it should end the same way.

The obstacles to be overcome are formidable. Old nations still adhere to traditional concepts, values and practices, while new nations brandish their fledgling sovereignty and demand change by any means. Rich and powerful states brace to protect their positions of prominence while the poor and weak cry out for equality and justice. Many of those who are tied by an ethnic or spiritual bond demand the unrestrained right to determine their own destiny. Terrorism and subversion are defended as legitimate means to attain legitimate goals. Diplomats who are entrusted with the terrible responsibility of preserving peace often see their primary goal to be the preservation of the interests of their own homeland. Short-term gain is frequently regarded as more important than long-term survival. Superpowers who glory in the perceived blessings of their own political system demonize their adversaries and insist upon the unlimited right to preserve or spread their vision to the inhabitants of all lands. The United Nations often appears as an impotent and biased debating society. The uncontrolled manufacture and sale of lethal arms continues, while weapons of mass destruction threaten to saturate the planet with seeds of death. Humankind stands poised on the brink of self-extinction. Yet, despite this gloomy picture, the light of hope can illuminate a brighter future if the heart and mind can find the way. It's an effort that must be made.

A. END THE ARMS RACE

In 1957, General Omar N. Bradley, who led the Allied armies to victory in Europe in World War II, addressed what he called "the central problem of our time." He saw that mankind was in desperate danger of destroying itself. In calling for peaceful accommodation, this American patriot appealed for "accord and compromise" in meeting "the most strenuous challenge to man's intellect." "I believe," he said, hopefully, "that we can somehow, somewhere, and perhaps through some as yet undiscovered world thinker and leader, find a workable solution."

We have postulated that international society as now structured lacks the essential components required to maintain a peaceful world. Creating a world order of acceptable codes, courts and enforcement mechanisms may take decades — or longer — to achieve. If we are to be realistic in seeking "a workable solution," we must make a distinction between short-range possibilities and long-range goals. As every Foreign Minister knows, the danger of nuclear explosion and the violence of on-going wars pose hazards that cannot wait for the arrival of evolutionary global panaceas. Fires that are burning must be contained or extinguished immediately — if possible. But if the community is not prepared to build a fire-station or to hire fire-fighters, it is to be expected that many conflagrations will not be brought under control and that black clouds — or raging infernos — will continue to darken the human horizon. All that can effectively be done in the short run is to contain the contemporary fires as best we can, while dilligently working toward a future day when all of the necessary parts can be put in place so that the House of Peace can rest on a firmer foundation than it does today. Let us consider some of the current antagonisms and conflagrations where — perhaps — the process of settling by compromise may hold some hope for "a workable solution" within the reasonably forseeable future.

Disarmament, being the most pressing problem, may be considered first. Certain actions may be possible which are consistent with the declared policies of both the Soviet Union and the United States and which do not jeopardize the national security of either state. The superpowers are already in agreement in principle that there should be universal and complete disarmament and that there should be essential equality between the two nations. It is common sense that where there is uncertainty about the destructive capability of each side, and a professed mutual desire to reduce armaments, the first thing that should be done is to seek some objective determination of the existing levels of different types of weapons. It may be recalled that the idea for an arms census as the logical starting point for a process of disarmament was proposed by France after World War II. There must be an impartial inventory of all weapons of mass destruction, taking into account not merely their numbers but also their condition, speed, location, deliverability, destructive capability, accuracy, vulnerability, and any other features that may determine their effectiveness in destroying human life. The publication of such a census would immediately demonstrate that — regardless of the nature or origin of the threat — the superpowers, with over 50,000 nuclear warheads are swamped with an overkill capacity that defies human reason.

Today, when radio and telecommunications are intercepted and monitored, and when satellites scan every inch of the planet and peer beneath the surface of the sea and land, most of the information about important weapons systems is already known. Mutual reporting requirements, accepted in SALT and other international accords, already supplement the satellite information. There are several impartial international agencies, such as the International Atomic Energy Agency, or the U.N. Disarmament Commission, that are ready and able to complete and verify a comprehensive international arms inventory. Their experts are qualified to compute the essential equivalents of asymetrical weapons and report significant imbalances. Where each side controls an arsenal that can destroy humankind many times over, the publication and proof of that mutual destructive power should serve to emphasize the urgency of arms control. Since both the Soviet Union and the United States possess large numbers of nuclear weapons that can be launched independently from hundreds of different locations on land, sea and air, knowledge of the adversary's power can only inhibit aggressive adventures by either side.

It is common sense that if disarmament is to be effective, it must be comprehensive. It makes no difference to the victim with which weapon his life, and that of his family, is snuffed out, or whether it was launched from beneath the soil, the sea, or the sky. Perhaps some procedural benefit may be derived from a temporary division of disarmament negotiations focusing on different types of weapons in different regions, but before significant progress can be expected, the frame of reference must be broadened to include the entire package of weapons of mass destruction. Fruitless disarmament efforts during the past decade have shown that different negotiators, meeting in different cities to negotiate different weapons (conventional, strategic or chemical) are more likely to multiply the problems than to resolve them. Each dedicated and determined negotiator feels impelled to demonstrate his ability to withstand compromise and to protect the stated position of his employer. What is needed is a top level policy decision that recognizes the need to compromise and makes it possible to move from stalemate to success. A balance of superpower weakness is far less menacing to the survival of humankind than a balance of power.

Once it is reasonably ascertained that each side has more than sufficient capacity to defend itself from any devastating surprise attack, the next logical step in a process of disarmament is to halt the continued manufacture of major weapons systems of every kind. It is common sense that one cannot reverse the direction of a train that is heading off the cliff without first bringing it to a stop. As part of the process of preventing further forward movement, there should be a comprehensive ban on the testing of all nuclear weapons — for any reason or in any area. In the words of former U.S. Under-Secretary of State, George Ball: "It should at least buy us time to bring a little rationality into the present lunatic nuclear arms race." A comprehensive test-ban treaty is in the making and has been widely endorsed by disarmament advocates everywhere. It should be adopted, ratified and respected.

The reduction of existing arsenals can then proceed by planned, coordinated and successive stages, with each step verified by an impartial control agency of the type suggested. Logically, the first reduction should be made by the nation found by impartial international experts to have the advantage, but it really makes no difference which party begins the process, since the excess on both sides is so enormous that no legitimate security interest is jeopardized during initial stages of disarmament. The nation that first moves to reduce its arms will be the first to gain good will. Once parity is reached, reductions must go hand in hand, until the goal is reached, as expressed by President Reagan on January 16, 1984: "To see the day when nuclear weapons will be banished from the face of the earth."

In meetings of the United Nations Disarmament Commission in 1984, a joint statement by India, Mexico, Tanzania, Sweden, Greece and Argentina appealed to all nuclear powers "to halt all testing, production and deployment of nuclear weapons and their delivery systems, to be immediately followed by substantial reductions of nuclear forces." The proposal was supported by many countries, including China and the Soviet Union. Dozens of distinguished American scientists and Nobel-Prize winners have recommended a comprehensive test ban, a non-proliferation policy, a bilateral freeze, no first use and massive reductions of nuclear arsenals. With so many people from so many different regions favoring major arms limitations, compromise should be possible.

The President of the United States, addressing the European Parliament on May 8, 1985, committed the United States not only to verifiable arms reduction agreements but also to a "sustained effort to reduce tensions and solve problems in its relations with the Soviet Union." He offered to exchange military observers at military exercises, to increase contacts between military leaders from both nations, to agree upon concrete confidence-building measures, to improve communications to reduce risk of misunderstanding in time of crisis, and to discuss the Soviet proposal for the non-use of force. These positive suggestions are further indications that it should be possible to move closer to reconciling divergent points of view.

One of the complications of arms reductions arises from the fact that both sides demand equality, which the Soviets describe as "equal security." But what constitutes "equal security" depends upon the subjective evaluation of Decision-Makers regarding the areas of risk faced by their nation. These differences in perspective — if they cannot be reconciled by negotiation — can perhaps be resolved by calling upon the services of objective and knowledgeable mediators. If litigants cannot agree, they may — as in every lawful society — have to turn to third-parties to resolve the dispute, and there are many suitable persons or agencies available to help maintain world peace. Absolute security for one nation means insecurity for others; reason and the spirit of compromise call for an accommodation.

The Soviet Union has made a number of specific proposals for the reduction of the existing level of arms as long as parity remains intact. One should consider the substance of the proposals — rather than the source — before reacting to them. Thus, the U.S.S.R. has indicated its willingness to accept complete and universal prohibition of nuclear weapons tests, limiting shipment and sale of conventional weapons to other countries, restricting military activity in the Indian Ocean (where nuclear submarines may safely hide), prohibiting deployment of weapons in outer space and banning the use of force in space or from space against earth. Soviet leaders have called for a non-aggression accord between NATO and Warsaw Pact nations and for a world treaty banning the use of force. They have proposed a weapons freeze and reductions of military spending. The U.S.S.R. has pledged not to be the first to use nuclear force and has condemned such use as an international crime. On October 4, 1983, Soviet Ambassador Troyanovsky called for "cessation, under effective verification, of the build-up of all components of nuclear arsenals, including all kinds of both delivery vehicles and weapons . . . and a halt to the production of fissionable materials for the purpose of creating arms." Neutron bombs and chemical weapons were also to be banned. All such offers are worthy of the most careful consideration. If the sincerity of the proponents is in doubt, they must be challenged to supplement their words by deeds which can be independently verified. Nothing constructive is achieved by brushing such proposals aside or denouncing them as "agitation propaganda." There should be restraint not only on aggressive arms, but also on aggressive tongues.

Significant progress has been made in the Vienna negotiations regarding the mutual and balanced reduction of conventional forces in Central Europe. Verification procedures via satellite monitoring and by checking points of troop departures have been agreed upon, and it has been recognized that it is not necessary that every single soldier be counted in order to arrive at a beneficial accord; a little more effort in the same direction should produce results satisfactory to both sides. Important understandings have also been reached by the Forty-nation Committee on Disarmament in Geneva regarding a comprehensive ban on chemical weapons and the destruction of production facilities and existing stockpiles under a system of on-site inspection. The Soviet Union and the United States have agreed in principle that the number of long-range strategic weapons must be significantly reduced, and some verification problems have been largely overcome. These, and similar, efforts can and must continue to be pursued with patience and flexibility.

Mikhail S. Gorbachev, after being appointed as the new General Secretary of the Communist Party, addressed the Central Committee on March 11, 1985, regarding U.S. — Soviet arms negotiations. His message was similar to the one given by his predecessor in 1984. Said Gorbachev:

> We do not strive to acquire unilateral advantages over the United States, over NATO countries, for military superiority over them; we want termination, and not continuation of the arms race and, therefore, offer a freeze of nuclear arsenals, an end to further deployment of missiles; we want a real and major reduction of the arms stockpiles, and of the development of ever new weapons systems, be it in space or on earth."

The arms-control goals expressed by the head of the Soviet Communist Party, when addressing those to whom he is responsible, do not sound very far removed from the declarations by the President of the United States. As the risk and burdens of increased weaponry become even more unbearable — a situation that is rapidly approaching — the possibilities for compromise should be enhanced. The biggest obstacle to nuclear arms control agreements has, purportedly, been the problem of verifying compliance. Yet, even here, the possibilities of settlement by compromise can be found. President Reagan's Commission on Strategic Forces — which employed the service of 2 former National Security Council Advisers, 4 former Secretaries of Defense, 3 former CIA Directors, and 2 former Secretaries of State — concluded: "The essential test of an effective verification system is that it will detect with a high degree of confidence any set of violations which would have significant impact on the strategic balance. The Commission believes that goal remains within our reach." The ABM Treaty provided for a Standing Consultative Commission to iron out disputes regarding compliance, and a similar mechanism — jointly or internationally appointed — can be used for other treaties. Allegations of non-compliance — often made by skeptics or those who oppose arms controls — should be subjected to careful public scrutiny. It will probably be found that the charges of violations by the adversary are exaggerated, while one's own violations are played down, or not mentioned at all. If the goal of effective verification "remains within our reach" — with a little more compromise — it should be possible to extend the reach until the goal comes within our grasp.

World military budgets approach two billion dollars per day; would it not be common sense to require that a tiny fraction of every military appropriation be used to study alternate means of protecting the national interest? The world's scientific brain power is squandered on weapons of mass destruction instead of being used for human betterment. Major powers — from East and West — sell billions of dollars worth of weapons to poor nations of the Third World, knowing that it will not eliminate violence but only make it more devastating. Imagine what would happen if the United States and the Soviet Union were blessed at the same time with leaders of vision and courage who would agree sincerely to implement their declared goal of complete disarmament under effective international controls. Imagine also that one half of the savings produced by the halt in arms production would be assigned to raising the standard of living in undeveloped countries, while the second half of the savings — amounting to many billions of dollars each year — would stimulate new industries, lower national debt, improve housing, education, medical care and provide similar social benefits to the citizens of both superpowers. Such a rational act of disarmament, even if taken in stages, would certainly be welcomed with wild enthusiasm among people all over the world and with an unprecedented outburst of affection and appreciation for both the United States and the Soviet Union for having begun to live up to their professed purpose of serving the interests of humankind. Would the national security of either the U.S. or the Soviet Union be diminished? Would the popularity of the national leader among his own people be reduced? Since the consequences of disarmament are so obviously desirable from every point of view, it is an insult to human intelligence to believe that such rational goals are unattainable.

B. CURB EXISTING CONFLICTS

What is almost as pressing as the need for nuclear disarmament is the need to halt or contain some of the ongoing military conflicts that continue to destroy or endanger the peace of nations. One of the potentially most explosive areas of conflict is the Middle East. It has been the scene of persistent strife ever since the United Nations — with support from both the Soviet Union and the United States — voted to create the State of Israel in 1948. The anguished cry of displaced Palestinians, longing to remain in their ancestral patrimony or to have an independent state of their own, mobilized the militant Arab world in support of their cause. In fruitless wars, the blood of young patriots drenched the desert sands. To break this bitter cycle of suffering and destruction, a number of measures that may encourage an acceptable compromise should be considered.

To begin with, greater efforts should be made to relieve the human indignity that prevails in some of the Palestenian refugee camps, in Lebanon, Israel and elsewhere. Living in a camp against one's will can be a dehumanizing experience. Improving conditions would not only make the lives of camp inhabitants more tolerable, but would help to diminish some of the discontent that breeds hatred like a festering wound. Millions of non-Arab refugees have, in recent years, been successfully resettled in all parts of the world. Even though western Germany was itself devastated by war, for example, it managed to relocate and absorb some nine million German-speaking refugees who readjusted to new and happy lives, with no thought of *revanchism*. Over a million Indo-Chinese have been aided in finding a new life in other countries. Even the poorest countries of Africa have welcomed large numbers of their fleeing neighbors as brothers and sisters. Masses of refugees from Afghanistan have been received by Pakistan, which shares the same religion and culture. Civilians in Central America, seeking to save themselves from the ravages of war, have also found homes in neighboring Latin countries. The U.N. High Commission for Refugees has satisfactorily resettled millions of people who now lead fairly normal lives. Humanitarian concern for Palestinian women and children who crowd squalid camps should motivate rich and sparsely-populated Arab nations to offer new homes to their co-religionists. Human beings should never be used as political pawns.

The legitimate demands of some four-and-a-half million Palestinians must somehow be satisfied. If the tragedy of the continuing conflict between Israelis and Palestinians is to be ended, a new initiative and direction is mandatory. Killing each other in recurring bouts of increasing savagery will bring only the peace of the dead; permanent tranquility requires that the Jews again make the Arabs their friends. The courageous Anwar Sadat demonstrated that peace between Egypt and Israel was possible through a process of accord and compromise —Israel returned occupied areas and a peace treaty was signed.

If autonomy for Palestinians within Israel, as envisaged by the Camp David Accords, or amalgamation with Jordan, does not prove feasible, another solution may be conceived. Oil-rich Saudi Arabia, in its own interest of preserving peace in the region, might offer a relatively tiny portion of its vast territory for the creation of an independent Palestinian state or autonomous political entity bordering on Jordan and the Red Sea. The territory of Saudi Arabia is more than a hundred times larger than the state of Israel, and only a tiny splinter would have to be earmarked for Palestinians. Jordan is already home to a million Palestinians and the two-and-a-half million Arab refugees who now live in Lebanon, Israel, Gaza, and the West Bank would not have far to move to be relocated in the new national home among neighbors who share a common language and religion. Israel might be required to pay compensation to the Saudis — a small price for permanent peace. The sacrifices entailed in such a minor realignment of borders and relatively modest resettlement program would be far less than the cost and suffering of incessant warfare. Terrorism and combat can only end if the causes of the discontent are eliminated.

If peaceful solutions are to be found, nations must not become stymied when difficulties are encountered; they must, instead, learn to build on progress that has already been made. We have seen that in several instances, when the Soviet Union and the United States were able to agree upon joint action, fighting in the Middle East was brought to a halt. The Security Council, by unanimous vote on November 22, 1967, adopted Resolution 242, affirming that a just and lasting peace in the Middle East required "withdrawal of Israel armed forces" and "acknowledgment of the sovereignty, territorial integrity and political independence of every state in the area and their right to live in peace within secure and recognized boundaries free from threats or acts of force." In 1973, Resolution 338, calling for immediate implementation of Resolution 242, who also unanimously adopted. Enduring peace can only be obtained if all of the real parties to a conflict are included in the settlement negotiations. What is called for now is a round-table conference of all of the warring parties and feuding factions that are willing to honor the principles approved by the international community.

If the superpowers are sincere in their desire to preserve human life, they will again insist upon a cease-fire and place an embargo on all arms into the area where fighting continues. Those who choose to continue on a course of violent conflict should be treated as brigands. It is inconceivable that they could long endure against the combined determination of both the Soviet Union and the United States. An overwhelming U.N. force, drawn from non-aligned nations, would, as we have indicated, be the most appropriate instrument for disarming any rebels and for guaranteeing the peace. Failure of either superpower to cooperate in measures of collective security in the Middle East would be a clear indicator that the recalcitrant partner prefers to play power politics with the lives of large numbers of human beings.

The war between Iran and Iraq may be an international fire that, realistically, will have to burn itself out — because the world community has neither the means nor the desire to quell or extinguish the conflagration. The fundamentalist religious revolution that swept over Iran in 1979 was seen as a threat to neighboring states that feared expansion of Shiite Muslim influence. In September, 1980, Iraq, claiming title to the oil-rich border province of Khizastan, launched an attack against Iran, expecting a quick military victory. But, as is so often the case in war, Iraq underestimated the power of its rival and the nationalistic fervor inspired by its religious leader, the Ayatollah Khomeini. Iran had significant oil revenues and armies of militant young Shiite fanatics who were willing and even eager to become martyrs in what they perceived to be a holy war that would earn them passage through the gates of heaven. Iran was quite prepared to export its fanatics to Syria and Lebanon to join the crusade against the Israelis. The Ayatollah had managed to antagonize the United States by his actions against American hostages and his incessant denunciations of America as "the Great Satan." The Soviets, sharing a lengthy border with Iran, were not inclined to see the further spread of Islamic influence or power. Iran's brutal repression of ideological and political dissidents, and Iraq's long record of oppression against minorities like the Kurds, managed to alienate people all over the world.

Several things can be done that might help to mitigate some of the hardships caused by the war between Iran and Iraq. If the arms-suppliers could be induced to embargo all weapons and reduce their military assistance to both of the belligerents it would certainly dampen the conflict. A boycott of oil imports from those at war would also restrict their combative capacity and might serve as a restraint. But this presupposes a deep concern for the victims, and a willingness to help curb the carnage. As long as there is no direct threat to the flow of oil out of the Persian Gulf, or to other vital interests, other nations are probably not inclined to risk their own resources to prevent Iraqis and Iranians from killing each other. The conflict, now in stalemate, will run its course and, like all wars, will eventually be brought to an end by compromise or defeat. Those who deplore this waste of hundreds of thousands of human lives may be encouraged to press for an early "accord and compromise" or for the long-range reforms of the international order that have been suggested.

As long as the Security Council is not prepared to take seriously the spirit behind the definition of aggression that was so meticulously worked out by so many special committees of experts, and as long as it is not willing to exercise its enforcement responsibilities under the Charter, other wars will also have to be fought until the combatants themselves recognize that the cost in human despair demands that some compromise be reached.

South Africa, which is torn by internal and external strife as a result of its racist policy of apartheid, is a fertile field for settlement by compromise. Even within the black community, opinions are divided. There are those who argue that punishing the white government by imposing economic sanctions is a moral as well as a political imperative; others note that the United States is dependent upon South Africa for many strategic minerals that are only available in that country or in the Soviet Union, and that the conditions of black South Africans would be worsened if American trade and industries were removed. A compromise proposed by Leon Sullivan, a black minister from Philadelphia, has been accepted by most American companies operating in South Africa. They have voluntarily agreed to accept the "Sullivan principles" which prohibit racial discrimination. Such companies set an example for others and help to establish new standards for all. Recent improvements in housing, wages and working conditions may be attributed to the influence of such actions and it is hoped that the continued pressure by South Africa's largest trading partner (the U.S.) may bring about the desired goals of equality for all without the devastating effects of mass violence. It is not common sense that the best way to make things better is to make them worse.

The international community as a whole should continue to urge that South African troops be withdrawn from Angola and Namibia, and that Cuban troops — even if invited by the government of Angola — should pack their bags and go home. Namibia must be allowed to be free and independent — which is its legal right. What the underdeveloped nations of Africa need more than anything else is economic aid and the opportunity to develop their own resources and institutions. The sooner the combatants accept a process of reconciliation and compromise, the sooner will they be able to begin constructive action for the welfare of their poverty-stricken countrymen.

Similarly, the battles that are being fought in Central America are the bitter fruits of poverty and ideological conflict. The people of the region have a long history of impoverishment and oppression. It is common sense that revolting conditions will invite revolt. But the United States is convinced that the Soviet Union is the moving spirit behind the spread of leftist regimes into the Western Hemisphere. It points to the Soviet-backed governments of Fidel Castro and the Marxist leadership of Nicaragua as the inspiration behind the attempt to overthrow the prowestern government of El Salvador. To counter the perceived penetration of communism, the United States is providing economic and military assistance to El Salvador. The U.S. is also "covertly" training and supporting guerilla forces in Honduras and Guatemala to help overthrow the Marxist Nicaraguans. These actions are justified by the United States as necessary to preserve freedom and democracy in the region. Action by the Security Council is blocked by the veto power of both the U.S. and the U.S.S.R.

It may be noted that there is an unsettling similarity between interventions by the United States and the condemned hegemonism of the Soviet Union in its sphere of influence. American invasions of Guatemala (1954), Cuba (1962), the Dominican Republic (1965), and Grenada (1983), for example, have been supported by reference to various "Doctrines" which are not far removed from similar "Doctrines" invented by the adversary. Nor have all of these efforts — if any — produced a freer, more prosperous and happier life for all of the citizens of the respective countries.

The bipartisan Kissinger Commission concluded that there could be no real security in Central America without economic growth and social justice. They called for democratic self-determination, economic and social development, and cooperation in making the regional system of collective security more effective. They favored increased U.S. pressure on El Salvador to end use of "death squads" as a means of eliminating political rivals. All of these recommendations are constructive and worthy of support. The Commission also recommended increased military aid to sustain the present government of El Salvador until the needed reforms could be put into place. Military intervention is never a solution to economic and social problems. A militaristic approach defeats a humanistic approach. President Betoncur of Colombia expressed the view, in 1983, that intervention by the superpowers can only encourage peasants to "leave their sowing to take up alien arms and to dig their own graves." The United Nations had declared — by consensus — that aiding armed bands to carry out acts of armed force against another state qualifies as an act of criminal aggression. Is it too much to ask the Soviet Union, which sponsored the definition of aggression, and the United States, which endorsed it, to honor its letter and spirit?

The Foreign Ministers of Colombia, Mexico, Venezuela and Panama — acting pursuant to Security Council authorization — have been trying to mediate the Central American disputes. After considerable effort, they drafted a comprehensive agreement known as "The Contadora Act on Peace and Co-operation in Central America." It contained the legal committments required to restore peace. They recommended that there be an inventory of arms and that foreign military advisors should leave. A verification and Control Commission was recommended to monitor and assure compliance. Civil liberties were to be protected. The greatest concern of the four Foreign Ministers was to achieve a "just balance that would satisfy the various and often conflicting interests in the complex panorama of the region." It represented an intensive effort "for conciliation and harmonizing of interests," and was based on their conviction that finding an effective solution to the grave problems which the Central American region was experiencing was "an inescapable imperative." The Act was welcomed by the OAS. The United States was not enthusiastic — citing concern about compliance by Nicaragua. The four Foreign Ministers declared on 9 January 1985: "It would be inadmissible to allow political intransigence and the use of force to stand in the way of dialogue and negotiation." The Contadora Group recognized the need for compromise. Their peaceful approach should be supported and vigorously pursued until an acceptable accord is reached; it is far more likely to benefit the poor people of the region than the further escalation of armed conflict.

In another area of the globe, the needs of the inhabitants should also be given precedence over the political ambitions of powerful neighbors. As a sign of respect for world public opinion, the Soviet Union should withdraw its troops from Afghanistan and allow that country to return to its previously friendly but non-aligned status. Those who are providing arms to the rebels should stop; those refugees who have fled the country should be allowed to return under guarantees that they will be safe and that they can pursue their own ethnicity or religious convictions in peace. In Southeast Asia, communist Vietnam continues to occupy Kampuchea, and Communist China and Communist Russia vie for power and position while denouncing hegemonism in other nations. Divided territories like Korea, Germany, or even the city of Berlin, are not likely to be reunited until there is a general accommodation between the superpowers. Whatever differences exist between these two great nations — as well as others — must be reconciled by negotiation through diplomacy or by such peaceful means as mediation or arbitration, as mandated by the U.N. Charter they have accepted. Is it not common sense that Decision-Makers should live up to their committments? In all situations of tension that threaten world security, the only solution that is consistent with the objectives of peace and humanity is to seek an accord by compromise.

Compromise is vital not only regarding disarmament and the curbing of existing international conflict but also concerning the emerging principles of international law and cooperation. We have noted the very significant progress that is already being made in developing new norms of conduct and in accepting the social obligations that pertain to being a member of one human family. The spirit of compromise that has made progress possible can be fostered by being aware that there are very few absolutes and that notions of what is right, wrong or appropriate will vary with time and circumstances; that awareness makes it easier to "see the other fellow's point of view" and — even if it is not shared — to find some way of reaching an accommodation in order that peace and better relations may prevail.

II. Educate and Organize for Peace

The leaders of the United States and the Soviet Union share the capacity to lead the world to a more rational structure of the international order and they must bear the main responsibility for the present polarization of nations. The importance of other great states —such as China, with its ancient traditions and its population of a billion people, or of India with its 700 million nationals of diverse cultures and its recognized leadership of non-aligned nations — should not be minimized. Japan, with its inspiring constitutional renunciation of force, its industrious citizenry and its creation of a strong democratic and industrial society, has many lessons it can teach the world and its influence can be a positive force for peace. France, England and other countries of Europe have been cradles of great civilizations that contributed enormously to the advancement of humankind. The Arab world, Latin America and the many countries of the vast continent of Africa will play an increasing part on the world stage; their views, values, needs and interests must be respected. All peoples — wherever they dwell and whatever may be their economic condition, religious orientation or ideology — are entitled to equal dignity and consideration. Common sense indicates, however, that if the powerful Soviet Union and the mighty United States were able to compromise and reconcile their differences, all of the other nations and peoples would be so relieved and so enriched that few of them would want to —and none of them would dare or be able to — block the road to peace.

Failure of the two superpowers to reach a sincere accord to end wars, or to seek a new arrangement to assure peace, dooms humankind to insecurity and fear. It throttles the hopes and energies of people everywhere and misapplies the earth's limited resources for useless weapons of destruction instead of keeping them for human betterment. As long as international adversaries are not able to resolve their conflicts by peaceful means, and there is no machinery for enforcing peaceful behavior, states and peoples will have no other alternative but to resort to armed might to preserve what they consider to be their vital interests — and large numbers of individuals who have no personal quarrel with each other will die in battle. Masses of innocent men, women and children will also perish. One must not overlook the real danger that even small conflicts may get out of control and trigger the nuclear holocauset that will bring human history to its end. Common sense indicates that it is wiser and safer to accept restraints needed for a peaceful future than to adhere to the unrestrained destructive patterns of the past. But, we must face the crux of the matter — what if the Soviet Union and the United States and other Decision—Makers still lack the political will to reach the necessary compromises? What then?

A. MOBILIZE WORLD OPINION

If government leaders are unable to meet the challenge of creating a peaceful world order, if they are so bound by prejudice or habit or blinded by fanatic ideology that they cannot reach agreement on clear and unambiguous minimum standards for decent behavior, if they cannot be convinced that they must resolve their differences by peaceful means, and if they cannot create the modalities for enforcing peace in the world, then it will be up to peace-loving people everywhere to take the action needed to achieve their peaceful goals. Obviously, this cannot be done quickly. But there are a number of constructive steps that can be taken.

To begin with, the people themselves must be educated for peace rather than war. It is essential to try to overcome the burden of traditional hostilities and the habit of identifying all of the inhabitants of a land with the policies of their government. Nothing constructive is achieved by fruitless belaboring of past antagonisms and misdeeds — many of which may have been generated by leaders who have long since passed from the scene. The dehumanization of great nations, the distortions, generalizations, simplifications and villifications which add nothing but additional venom to a poisoned situation should be brought to a halt. The "confidence-building-measures" that have been accepted in principle by both the United States and the Soviet Union must be strengthened. Communication networks between the two nations and their citizens can be extended and used for common dialogue. Increased information, cultural and educational exchanges, and additional contacts between the people of both nations can help to "de-Satanize" false images that have been created for political reasons. Human beings can be taught to recognize that all human beings — even those who live in an alien land — are humans.

An example of beneficial cooperation can be found in the private meetings that have been taking place in Moscow since 1983 between an alliance of lawyers in the United States and their Russian counterparts, for the purpose of open dialogue regarding the urgent problems of nuclear arms control. American delegates, headed by Harvard Professors Roger D. Fisher and Abram Chayes, have met with representatives of the Association of Soviet Lawyers and have been able to agree upon joint statements. Agreements could be reached on a number of broad common principles, but even if no specific "victories" could be scored, the fact that a free and open discussion was possible is itself an essential stepping stone toward better understanding. Many other groups of concerned citizens from many lands are visiting the Soviet Union to compare opinions — and a few Soviet delegations are also travelling across the United States for the same purpose. All such efforts at understanding and education should be encouraged.

Student exchanges, particularly among those whose nations may be in conflict, should also be stimulated. Changes in the educational curricula must be made in order to demonstrate that there are dangerous limits to the present organization of world society — and that there are viable alternatives. Students on all levels must be helped to develop logical and ethical perceptions. Teachers must be taught to teach peace. As Mary E. Finn wrote in the Journal of Peace Research (Ohio: Kent State Univ., 1984): "When young people see that there are adults who work to resolve conflicts peaceably, they may be more hopeful about there being a future for them."

There must be an end to the glorification of killing and violence. Children must be taught that it is far nobler to live for humankind than to die for the glory of a particular ruler or sect. Young men should not be willing to die for old slogans. Peace studies should become part of the curriculum of all schools. All great religions and cultures are built on respect for order and justice, and religion can expand its moral and ethical teachings to insist that nations develop and accept the procedures and institutions needed for a peaceful world society. The typical twenty-one gun salute should not be regarded as a fitting tribute to visiting heads of state — a bevy of pigeons for peace or a greeting by singing children would be far more appropriate for modern times. The 1983 Pastoral Letter on War and Peace issued by the U.S. Bishops of the Catholic Church, and proclamations by the World Council of Churches — to say nothing of the educational efforts of the B'hai, Quakers and pacifist groups — are fine examples of theological involvement in the role of peacemaker. The Union of Concerned Scientists speaking for thousands of members of the scientific community, has a comprehensive program to help educate the American public on the effects of nuclear war. They produce a steady stream of valuable books, reports, studies, briefing materials and films.

When it comes to educating their people, smaller nations must not allow themselves to be intimidated or bullied by more powerful ones. The non-aligned nations that represent two-thirds of humankind may be weak in arms, but they are a powerful moral and spiritual force. Their 1983 message is worth recalling:

> The earth belongs to us all — let us cherish it in peace and true brotherhood, based on the dignity and equality of man.

It is a message to be respected and repeated. All of the modern instrumentalities that help to mold public opinion — the schools, the church, press, television and other information media, as well as private organizations and individuals — must be mobilized to nudge the world along the path to peace.

Admittedly, it is much easier to educate for peace in democratic societies where there is a high level of literacy and freedom of opinion and expression. In the closed or controlled régimes of totalitarian states — whether of the Right or Left — those who might be able to influence public opinion may not dare to espouse policies or practices that transgress the official doctrines of those in power. Nonetheless, the days when it was possible to have a hermetically sealed society are over, and there is no country on earth that would dare to oppose peace as an objective of government. Surely, the common people everywhere long for nothing more than to live their lives in tranquility and dignity. A bridge of understanding must be built to unite all those who share these common human aspirations. Teachers and other educators — from parents to preachers — must have the courage of their convictions; their lives and the lives of future generations may depend upon it. Silence may be more dangerous than speaking out for peace.

The expansion of international trade, increased cooperation in economics, science and technology, and in coping with common environmental problems is not only mutually beneficial but also serves as a medium of education. "Peaceful coexistence" — the policy favored by the Soviet Union, China and many other nations — is not a dirty word. As Henry Kissinger has pointed out in his book *American Foreign Policy:*

> We are compelled to coexist. We have an inescapable
> obligation to build jointly a structure for peace. Recognition
> of this reality is the beginning of wisdom for a sane and
> effective foreign policy today.

"Peaceful collaboration" in furthering the rights and welfare of all human beings is a more positive goal that can be taught in schools throughout the world.

Individuals and institutions must be organized for peace. The power of the masses, if properly marshalled and motivated, should never be underestimated — as Ghandi and other leaders have demonstrated. Young people in the United States proved that they could change a government and halt a war by determined peaceful protests against the inhumanity of U.S. actions in Vietnam. The history of dictatorial régimes that have been ousted by an aroused citizenry is ample evidence that the radiations of widespread discontent are capable of penetrating and crumbling even the walls of totalitarian repression. Each concerned citizen has a role to play. What that role may be will depend upon individual interests and capabilities. Some may only be able to express an opinion in private, others may cast a vote, write a letter, sign a petition or write a book. Some may lead or join a march, make a speech, teach a class or make a cash or other contribution to the worthy cause. Each person has an obligation to try to maintain peace today and for future generations and to take such nonviolent measures toward that end as may be within his or her power. Those who favor peace — and who understand the specifics of what is needed to build a more orderly society — must encourage every action that moves humankind toward the desired goal. They must oppose everything that impedes the movement toward a more tranquil future. Persistent expressions (in whatever form) of concern, anguish or wrath do not fall only on deaf ears. A Czech refugee, Josef Korbel, writing on *Détente in Europe,* said:

> The hunger for freedom has deepened and men will not be silenced forever. In what year or decade this will happen, no one can say. But it will happen.

Throughout the world there are thousands of non-governmental organizations and other institutions, and private groups of various size, composition and strength, concerned with one or more facets of the problem of world peace. Many of them are dedicated to resolving one specific issue — such as disarmament or U.N. reform. Most of them are inadequately funded and they lack coordination and cooperation with similar agencies with compatible goals. These many loose strands now float on a vast sea. If they are to catch and hold the elusive prize of peace, they must be drawn together and woven into a powerful and coordinated network. Modern computer technology and communication techniques now make it possible to reach out across the nation and across the world in ways that were never possible in the past. An international brotherhood of citizens who are concerned with the problems of peace can and should be formed to break the back of "politics-as-usual." The combined intellectual and persuasive force of such a coalition could overwhelm the ideologists who now breed a philosophy of militarism, fear and hate.

Many new institution are being formed that can play a very useful role in educating for peace. "Peace Studies" are beginning to flower in universities all across the land. Many institutions in Europe are dedicated to peace research and private foundations support such activities in other parts of the world a well. A United Nations University began operating in Tokyo in 1975. A University for Peace was established in Costa Rica in 1983. A peace institute in honor of President Harry Truman exists at the Hebrew University in Jerusalem. In 1985, the U.S. Congress declared that America must create a U.S. Institute of Peace and millions of dollars were authorized to support educational activities to further the twin goals of national security and international peace. As has been pointed out by Robert Muller, Assistant Secretary-General of the United Nations, in his book *New Genesis:* "Global education must prepare our children for the coming of an interdependent, safe, prosperous, friendly, loving, happy planetary age as has been heralded by all great prophets." "To reach peace, teach peace."

In a New York Times Magazine article in December, 1984, Professor Robert W. Tucker of the John Hopkins School of Advanced

International Studies in Washington D.C. wrote: "The public will not support a policy that does not hold out the hope of improvement in our relationship with the Soviet Union, and that does not actively seek improvement." He argues for a diplomacy of conciliation in order to preserve a domestic consensus and allied support. He argues that the Reagan Administration, having reasserted American military strength, is now in a better position to seek a modest and realistic understanding with Russia. His conclusions reflect the prevailing political pressures that have been generated in the cause of peace.

The proposals and suggestions that have been mentioned here are not intended to offer definitive or exclusvie answers to all of the perplexities involved in restructuring our present violent international society into a more tranquil one. Many other plans and ideas are deserving of very careful consideration and debate. Robert Johanson, for example, President of the Institute for World Order, has analyzed U.S. Foreign Policy in a book, *The National Interest and the Human Interest* and has suggested alternative policies that are likely to lead to peace. Former U.S. Ambassador George Kennan has written extensively, calling for massive cuts in weaponry and warning that the present policies of our government will lead us over the precipice "like lemmings heading for the sea." Gerald and Patricia Mische, founders of Global Education Associates have looked beyond the national security straitjacket in their book *Toward a Human World Order*. Dyson Freeman has written a number of perceptive articles on "Weapons and Hope" in the New Yorker magazine of 1984. Johan Galtung has been a frequent contributor of new ideas, as evidenced by his latest book in 1984 *There are Alternatives: Four Roads to Peace and Security*. Professor Louis Sohn has for many years been in the forefront of those who have been making constructive suggestions on ways to render the international order more effective and more responsive to human needs. These are only a few names from what could be an enormous catalogue of concerned and able citizens whose only objective is to improve the condition of the world. Hanna and Alan Newcombe, founder of the Canadian Peace Research and Education Association, have for many years been publishing extracts of ideas for peace that have originated all over the globe. It is only through such a process of universal education — the advancement and challenging of new ideas —that the difficult problems of improved social engineering can be overcome. What is required is that the agile and idealistic minds of people everywhere apply themselves in an organized and coordinated way to mastering the complexities of transforming the present world order. The genius of the human intellect will find the most suitable solutions. If world public opinion can be educated for peace, it is common sense that — in time — the will of the people can alter the will of the politicians.

B. CREATE A COUNCIL FOR PEACE

If the U.N. Security Council remains ideologically divided, unwilling or unable to carry out its assigned responsibility, and if the General Assembly continues as a debating society that frequently places national interests above international interests, it will be necessary for the people of the world to look elsewhere for their guidance on the complicated issues of war and peace. It should be possible to establish a permanent council of independent and knowledgeable scholars and statesman, recruited from all areas of the world and representative of a wide diversity of ideological and cultural traditions, who will consider the issues that threaten world security and who will be able to recommend appropriate solutions that will be least disruptive of human life and values. We must learn to accept a pluralistic world that draws its creative strength from living in peaceful diversity rather than under the terror of competing superpowers.

Unfortunately, one cannot rely on national leaders alone or on official statements. Propaganda to support political objectives is part of the political arsenal of all states. Even within governments, there are competing groups; each side seeks to obtain support for its own position and makes arguments designed for that purpose. This is true not only in dictatorial régimes. J. William Fulbright — who for many years was Chairman of the Foreign Relations Committee of the U.S. Senate — upon reaching his 80th year — was asked what he had learned. His reply, according to the New York Times, was: "Not to trust government statements . . . They fit the facts to fit the policy." Those who would know the truth must look beyond the halls of the United Nations or the capitols of competing states.

Over the years, a number of *ad hoc* groups have been constituted to cope with the frightening security problems faced by the world community. These have usually been composed of distinguished citizens whose objectivity and dedication to human welfare could hardly be challenged. The Club of Rome, the Brandt Commission, the Inter— American Dialogue and the Trilateral Commission are illustrative. Perhaps the best recent example can be found in the work of the Independent Commission on Disarmament and Security Issues, under the Chairmanship of Olof Palme, a former Prime Minister of Sweden. Among the seventeen members of the Commission were former U.S. Secretary of State Cyrus Vance, David Owen, the United Kingdom's former Prime Minister, Salim Salim, the Minister of Foreign Affairs of Tanzania, Alfonso Garcia-Robles, the former respected Foreign Minister of Mexico and persons who had occupied high office in Japan, India, Holland and other nations. Giorgi Arbatov, a full member of the Central Committee of the Communist Party of the U.S.S.R., was also one of the Commissioners. They were supported by a distinguished staff of scientific advisers and consultants. Their primary goal was to seek the basis for disarmaments agreements and to stimulate informed public debate on the issues of war and peace. Between 1980 and 1982, they held a dozen meetings in cities throughout the world — Vienna, Moscow, Mexico, Paris, Tokyo, Bonn, New York, Oxford and Stockholm. In the Prologue to their final report: *Common Security, A Blueprint for Survival,* Cyrus Vance wrote:

> There is one overriding truth in this nuclear age — no nation can achieve true security by itself. . . There are no real defenses against nuclear armed missiles — neither now nor in the foreseeable future. . . Security in the nuclear age *means* common security. This has been the central conclusion of our commission.

The former Secretary of State referred to the weakness of the present international system "because it lacks a significant structure of laws and norms of behavior." He noted that "governments have not permitted the U.N. to function as it should." These practical politicians, when confronted with the realities of the world in which we live, made a number of specific suggestions to move toward a more secure world. Their views and proposals were consistent with what has been suggested in this book: curb the arms race through a comprehensive test ban treaty, begin a downward spiraling of arms, strengthen the role of the U.N. and its peace-keeping capabilities, expand nuclear-free zones and enhance economic progress. Olof Palme warned about waiting "for the initiatives of governments and experts." "It will only come about," he said, "as the expression of the political will of peoples in many parts of the world."

American business leaders have been called upon to lead the way out of the current impasse between the nuclear powers. Howard Willens, in his 1984 book *The Trimtab Factor — How Business Executives Can Help Solve the Nuclear Weapons Crisis,* quoted President Eisenhower's 1959 statement: "I think that people want peace so much that one of these days governments had better get out of the way and let them have it."

Such independent studies indicate that a properly constituted Permanent Council for Peace, composed of renowned thinkers, spiritual, community and business leaders, would be unencumbered by the political intrigues that now hamper the effectiveness of governments and the United Nations — it could be free of the ideological biases that now block solutions to many international problems. Its views — or those of similar sub-committees in different regions — could be vigorously disseminated through all of the modern means of communication as well as through the many institutions dedicated to a tranquil world. The organization, staffing, and funding for such an independent Permanent Council for Peace should present no insuperable administrative problems. It requires no more than a handful of men and women with minds of broad and compassionate sweep who are known to be dedicated to a peaceful world of law and justice. Such respected and renowned personalities as Pope John Paul II, Perez de Cuellar (after he retires from the U.N.,) Tommy Koh of Singapore (who did an exemplary job as President of the Final Conference on the Law of the Sea,) Professor Bengt Broms of Finland (who dealt effectively with reaching a definition of aggression by consensus and who has been dealing with Charter reform,) or many other leaders from small states that have never threatened anyone. These, and many others, could make very suitable candidates. Operational funds could be solicited from individuals as well as private organizations and foundations. But it would have to be made very clear in the Constitution for the Council for Peace that it must remain independent in reporting truthfully on all problems that threaten peace and in its commitment to the goals of universal brotherhood for all peoples. Such a Council could also serve as a mediator to help conflicting parties to resolve their differences by peaceful means — without having to rely exclusively on an over-burdened Secretary-General of the U.N. It could offer long-range vision and planning and could be an inspiration as well as a guide to all peacelovers.

It is not my purpose to suggest all of the details for such an organization, but merely to indicate the broad outline and to argue that the people of the world may have to go beyond the usual framework of looking only to their own national leaders as the source of information or direction regarding the conflicts that jeopardize all of humankind. A Permanent Council for Peace — backed by an educated and organized public — would speak with a very powerful voice. Using all of the modern public relations techniques, it should be easier to "sell" peace than it is to "sell" war. A determined international campaign of truth and wisdom, led by a Council of dedicated, knowledgeable and distinguished world citizens, could go over the heads of governments to reach the eyes, ears, hearts and minds of people everywhere.

III. See the Total Picture: Summary and Review

One of the difficulties in moving toward world peace is the failure of Decision-Makers — and others — to see the total picture and to recognize that everything is interrelated. Progress in attaining one component stimulates acceptance of other components; conversely, failure to advance in one area impedes progress elsewhere. The evolutionary pattern has been sketched in order to reveal the entire panorama. The fact that some of the arguments presented here may have been made elsewhere does not diminish their validity but reinforces them. I rely not merely on the weight of authority but primarily upon the reader's common sense. Humankind is not simply moving in a vicious circle but is on an upward spiral. True, there are times of erratic and depressing gyration but that is not cause for despair. If the will can be generated to build the future on the mistakes of the past, the forward movement toward a more rational world will continue.

A. EVERYTHING IS LINKED

As we briefly perused the pages of history, we detected the gradual evolution of new concepts that arose to meet changing social needs. Beginning with ancient times, we saw the early origins of rules and codes for the conduct of tribes and nations, and the development of institutions for the settlement of commercial disputes without the use of force. General principles for peaceful behavior were articulated, and primitive international law was born as a means of preserving order in a growing world society. In 1648, at Westphalia, the contemporary system of independent sovereign states was created. Soon thereafter, new plans were drafted for an improved restructuring of the international system. The "Grand Designs" and the ideas they generated spanned the oceans and seved as a foundation for the establishment of a new commonwealth — the United States of America. As conflicts in Europe continued, and the burden of arms required to maintain a balance of power became increasingly unbearable, European nations convened for the first disarmament conference in 1899. Instead of programs to limit arms, or ensure peace, sovereign states were not prepared to go beyond formulating rules for a modicum of humanitarianism in war. Detailed legal codes and statutes for international courts were meticulously prepared by respected legal experts, but they were rejected by political leaders. Humankind — engulfed in the first world war — paid dearly for the inability of Decision-Makers to overcome entrenched traditions.

Revulsion against the agonies cause by World War I inspired nations, for the first time, to join together in a League of Nations that, hopefully, would be able to maintain the peace. Some of the organizers pointed out that what was required was an international legislature to enact laws binding upon all, a judicial method for settling disputes peacefully, control of national armaments and a coordinated system of sanctions or an international army to enforce rules of conduct accepted by common consent. The importance of social justice to tamp the fires of discontent was also recognized.

The covenant that was finally adopted by the Decision-Makers embraced some, but not all, of the elements necessary for the effective control of internatinal violence. The inability of the United States to become a member of the League doomed the new-born association to an early demise; but — as we have noted — there were other contributing factors that rendered the first world organization incapable of fulfilling its aspirations. The infant body was finally allowed to perish by the unwillingness of its members to nourish it with the support that was needed. The 1919 efforts to apply international criminal law to deter future aggression and crimes of war were soon aborted. Taking only part of the medicine could not cure the ills of an ailing international society. Being unwilling to shoulder the risks and burdens of maintaining peace, nations soon found themselves embroiled in the flames of World War II.

The tragedy of the second world conflagration increased the

determination of the victors to form a new international organization that would be more successful in ending the scourge of war. After the allied victory in 1945, the United States — then the most powerful nation on earth — took the lead in confirming that aggression was an international crime, for which responsible leaders could be tried and punished. The U.S. also seized the initiative in drafting a charter for the proposed new world association. Both the United States and the Soviet Union insisted that each of the organizers must have the right to veto any proposed enforcement action. Everyone knew that the effectiveness of the Charter depended upon the ability of the major powers — despite ideological differences — to be able to work together in harmony. Once again, nations had taken a step forward. It was as far as they could go at the time. But, once again, it did not go far enough.

Decision-Makers were unwilling to create a system of effective economic sanctions or an international military force to maintain peace. The inability of international society to accept adequate restraints or to adopt clear and binding rules and effective machinery for the peaceful settlement of disputes, inevitably led to inordinate human suffering throughout the globe. Since the end of World War II, Asia has seen major conflicts; Africa has been torn by violence; the American hemisphere has been in constant turmoil; the Middle East has not tasted peace; and other regions periodically erupt in bloody battle. The principal victims were innocent people of many lands, divided by no personal hostility, but united by a common human desire to live in peace and dignity. Despite the cost in human suffering, the use of force almost invariably failed to produce any enduring benefit.

In PART TWO, we mentioned some of the things that *should* be done to improve the international order. In negotiating acceptable standards of international behavior, nations and their leaders should learn to be more tolerant of differences, recognizing that all values are relative and subject to change. There must be a willingness to compromise without being compromised. Vituperation is no substitute for patient persuasion. Agreements should be unambiguous so that those who will not accept or conform to common norms may be identified, isolated, condemned and sanctioned. In matters that affect international security, the sovereignty of international law should take precedence over the sovereignty of the national state. Acceptance of what I have described as the "judicial role" should include reliance upon every form of peaceful settlement. It is no longer tolerable that international differences should be resolved by the use of national might. Nations should be required to honor their pledges to the U.N. Charter, and particularly to its prohibition against the use of force. An International Criminal Court, to deter aggression and other international crimes and to punish those who flout the laws of humanity, is an essential component of the recommended judicial system.

International law enforcement is the most difficult and the most undeveloped leg of the triad (codes, courts and enforcement) needed for a peaceful society. Effective enforcement requires:

A — An improved organization of international society, including increased efficiency of the United Nations, better cooperation within the Security Council and greater regional coordination.

B — Universal and complete disarmament. This is most imperative. Its difficulty is compounded by the fact that secrecy and complicated technology makes the public dependent upon "experts" who may have parochial or economic interests that run counter to the stated objective. Nuclear weapons are simply not an acceptable means of deterring war, since they must lead to competitive escalation and the risk of mutual annihilation. The testing and production of all nuclear weapons should be banned and there should be a gradual, and joint, reduction of existing nuclear arsenals under effective and impartial international controls until all such weapons are destroyed. Pending the elimination of all weapons of mass destruction, nuclear-free zones should be expanded, and non-nuclear states should receive interim guarantees protecting their security. Arms of all kinds must be viewed as one totality and their numbers and destructive capability measured and publicized by an impartial census as a prelude to lowering the level of all means of human immolation.

C — Sanctions must be organized and coordinated on an international basis. The existing catalogue of the world's resources and the interdependence of all nations makes it possible for economic sanctions to be more effective now than ever before. Where peaceful means of coercion prove inadequate, they should be augmented, as a last resort, by the use of an international military force. This was part of the original U.N. plan and nations should not be allowed to evade obligations they have freely accepted.

D — Social justice is the final prerequisite if there is to be peaceful compliance with international law. It must continue to be enhanced.

The requirements that have been outlined — codification of law, courts with authority to resolve disputes, and enforcement made possible by improved international machinery, disarmament, sanctions, an international peace force and social justice — are the essential stones in the arch of peace. Each one must be set in its proper place if the structure of international peace is to be sustained.

These essential components of a rational world order are all intertwined and dependent upon each other. Clarification of norms of international behavior encourages acceptance of judicial authority, which — in turn — contributes toward the effective functioning of the international order. More international cooperation diminishes the need for massive weaponry, encourages disarmament and allows enforcement to be taken over by economic sanctions or an international peace force. The reduction of national arsenals makes funds available to meet social demands that give rise to political unrest. Combined, these measures promote an international system in which clear laws and judicial tribunals encourage the peaceful settlement of disputes and offer a more secure and enriched human life for everyone. Each segment is a vital link in a chain that must be forged if world peace is to be secured.

B. NO CAUSE FOR DESPAIR

To focus — as some so-called "realists" do — on the shortcomings of nations without reminding the reader of those areas of social interaction where significant progress has been made, is to paint a bleak and distorted picture. Exaggerated criticism and emphasis on frailties of the international structure engenders cycnicism and skepticism; it erodes the public confidence needed to stimulate the improvements that are required. It is far more useful — and accurate — to recognize what has been accomplished, so that it may form a firmer base upon which to build the many structures that are still needed to make the international system more effective. During the past few decades, unprecedented strides have been made but there are still major shortcomings — there can be no cause for satisfaction or complaceny. There is also no cause for despair. As we peruse some of the significant advances during this brief period, one should recognize that each one was a step taken for the first time since man began to walk the face of the earth.

Unbridled national sovereignty is being gradually restricted by the need for coping with common problems on a global basis. Binding international rules govern the environment and outer space. New international tribunals have been created to deal with a host of special problems which — by agreement of sovereign nations — are settled only. by peaceful means. The processes of mediation and conciliation are being improved. Disenchantment with the visibile weaknesses of the United Nations Organization has led to persistent demands for reform — both inside and outside the U.N. there is a growing awareness of the need for improvements. The growth of regionalism and the alignment of many nations to protect or further their common interests is evidence of the evolutionary trend toward a consolidation of the international order.

In the field of disarmament, some progress has been noted and more people are coming to realize that unless we destroy all weapons of mass destruction, the weapons will destroy us all. New peacekeeping mechanisms and forces are slowly being developed. Multinational cooperation and increasing humanitarian concern is a reality of international life. Although the lights of progress flicker and grow dim from time to time, the trend toward an integrated, coordinated and more humane world is clearly discernable to the penetrating eye.

The most compelling stimulus today toward a peaceful world under law is the fact that there are no rational alternatives. Rival nations seething with hostility now possess weapons capable of destroying all living things — such power is no longer a safeguard, it is a menace. Mandatory settlement of all international differences by peaceful means is not a matter of idealism but of self-interest, survival and common sense. Unilateral and unfounded denunciations of the adversary as a demon to be slain by a self-styled savior are as unreal and unreasonable as they are dangerous and intolerable; particularly since those who are to be smitten are usually not the guilty ones but innocent and peaceloving bystanders. In the conflict between communism and capitalism, humanism must not become the first victim.

If people will use their common sense, certain truths will become self-evident. As we noted at the outset, every town, hamlet, and city —all over the world and for at least hundreds of years — has agreed to be governed by a system of laws, courts and enforcement procedures. Admittedly, the results are less than perfect, but of this we can be sure — even an imperfect system is infinitely better than the anarchy and chaos that would be prevail if there were no laws, no courts and no police to enforce rules of behavior. Yet, in the international sphere, sovereign states are bound by very few laws, the international court system (such as it is) lacks the powers of ordinary tribunals and international enforcement is all but absent. Common sense dictates that even though the international scene is much more complicated than the domestic one, the model that has been found to be essential to regulate every smaller political entity should also be applicable to govern relations among nations. In an interdependent world, it makes little sense for nations to pretend that they are completely independent. Common sense should tell us that in today's dependent world the notion of absolute sovereignty is obsolete.

It is also common sense that those who purport to believe in the rule of law should support clarification of international laws and the strengthening of the international judicial system. If the international community decrees that there are international crimes, such as terrorism and hostage-taking, it is only common sense that there should be courts to punish the criminals. It is common sense that nations claiming to support the rule of law should accept the jurisdiction of an international court of justice. It is common sense that those who wish to live under the protection of law cannot seek protection in lawlessness.

It is common sense that you cannot stop an arms race without stopping the production of arms. If one wishes to determine the relative military power of nations, it makes sense to seek an objective inventory of all the world's armaments, including an expert estimate of the destructive capability of different weapons systems. If it is confirmed that the capacity to destroy human life exceeds the number of human beings available to be killed, it makes no sense to continue to expand the superflous destructive capacity. Furthermore, if nuclear weapons are not usable because they would destroy all civilization, then it is only common sense to ask: "of what use are such non-usable weapons?" The theory of deterrence through Mutual Assured Destruction is based on the MAD logic that if a nation remains vulnerable it remains safe. Those who support the argument that armaments are essential for deterrence often cite the classical Latin adage: "If you want peace, prepare for war." But ancient Rome did not anticipate the nuclear age, and history has shown that those who prepared for war usually got what they prepared for. Common sense prescribes: "If you want peace, prepare for peace!" It is common sense that it is better to replace a system of Mutual Assured Destruction by a system of Mutual Assured Survival.

Just as no private citizen would surrender his arms if he had an armed and belligerent neighbor in an area where laws, courts and police were non-existent, so too, no nation can be expected to forego reliance on its own military might as long as there are no other means available for maintaining justice and peace. Common sense should tell us that if we want to stop the stockpiling of nuclear death, we must establish a system where national arms will no longer be needed for national defense. It is more sensible, and much cheaper, to eliminate nuclear missiles than to try to build an impenetrable shield in outer space which — hopefully — will intercept most of the incoming nuclear bombs before they innundate the target with a lethal shroud. No one can expect to eliminate all differences among nations or peoples (or even families,) but where the alternative is to die for those differences, common sense suggest that one must try — and it should be possible —to find a tolerable way for both sides to live with those differences.

It has repeatedly been noted that there is no quick or facile solution to the problems of world peace. Ingrained mistrust and ancient hatreds cannot be dissolved overnight. Nor can competing religions, cultures, values or political ideologies be suddenly reconciled. There is no easy revolution and no instant evolution. A new structure of international society is slowly being born, and — like all births it may be accompanied by pain and suffering. The obligation of concerned citizens is first to try to understand what needs to be done and then to do everything in their power to move in the right direction, in the hope that a more enlightened international order will be able to enrich all of humankind. There is no reason to lose heart.

At an unofficial conference in the spring of 1985, former U.S. Presidents Gerald Ford and Jimmy Carter invited a number of experts and representatives from the Soviet Union and the United States and other lands to consider the arms problem. It was generally concluded that past arms agreements had been negotiated in good faith and that —with a few technical violations by both sides — the accords had been honored. Jimmy Carter came away convinced "that even the more contentious issues could be resolved by the superpowers in a mutually satisfactory way." He felt that if the President could frame future accords as "executive agreements" approval by the Congress could be done by majority vote without the necessity for two-thirds vote of the Senate that had members who "are philosophically opposed to any reasonable agreement" — and the path might thereby be cleared for further progress.

Leaders of the two most powerful nations on earth — those to whom this book is dedicated — have (as we have noticed) given public assurances in the forum of the U.N. that they are ready and eager to move towards the goals here indicated as being essential for a peaceful world. Soviet Foreign Minister Gromyko, addressing the General Assembly in 1984, acknowledged that world problems "cannot be solved by force." He favored "prompt measures to reduce and eventually eliminate nuclear weapons altogether." He saw both the possibility and necessity for raising the level of trust and for easng tensions among states. He called for "general and complete disarmament" as he appealed for peace and "normal relations with the United States." He promised Soviet cooperation with all nations to help ease tensions and create an atmosphere of trust. Mikhail Gorbachev's policy statement to his own Central Committee on March 11, 1985 (previously quoted) was further confirmation of Soviet willingness to end the arms race.

President Reagan, in 1983, publicly acknowledged: "A nuclear war cannot be won and must never be fought." When he addressed the U.N. General Assembly again in 1984, he pointed to the new ties between the United States and China as evidence that the American government was willing to improve relations with countries that were ideologically different. "The United States welcomes diversity and peaceful competition," he said. He acknowledged that there was no sane alternative to arms control and he outlined there objectives of U.S. — Soviet relations:

1 — "To reduce and eventually to eliminate the threat and use of force in solving international disputes."

2 — "To reduce the vast stockpiles of armaments," and

3 — To establish "greater cooperation and understanding" between the United States and the Soviet Union. His closing comments echoed the sentiments expressed throughout this book:

> For the sake of a peaceful world, a world where human dignity and freedom is respected and enshrined, let us approach each other with tenfold trust and thousandfold affection. A new future awaits us. The time is here, the moment is now.

The President of the United States concluded his statement with a quotation from Tom Paine, the author of *Common Sense:*

"We have it in our power to begin the world over again."

REFERENCES

Many of the citations and documents mentioned in the text may be found in the author's previously published books of commentary and documents: *Defining International Aggression — The Search for World Peace* (2 volumes); *An International Criminal Court — A Step Toward World Peace* (2 volumes); *Enforcing International Law — A Way to World Peace* (2 volumes). [Published by Oceana Publications, Dobbs Ferry, N.Y., 1975, 1980, 1983.]

Only additional citations or works of particular interest are noted herein.

PART ONE: WHAT *HAS* BEEN DONE

H.S. Maine, *Ancient Law* (N.Y.: Scribners, 1864).

S.A. Korff, "An Introduction to the History of International Law" 18 AJIL* (1924) p. 252.

C. Van Vollenhoven, *The Law of Peace* (London: Macmillan, 1936).

Elihu Root, "The Codification of International Law" 19 AJIL* (1925) p. 675.

The Classics of International Law, published by the Carnegie Endowment, for works by Francisco de Vitoria, Hugo Grotius and Samuel Pufendorf; available on microfilm from Oceana.

S. Rosenne, *The Progressive Codification of International Law* (1925-1928), League of Nations Committee of Experts for the Progressive Codification of International Law (N.Y.: Oceana, 1972) 2 volumes.

Yearbook of the International Law Commission (N.Y.: U.N., 1949-   ).

United Nations Juridical Yearbook (N.Y., U.N., 1962-   ).

R.F. Clarke, "A Permanent Tribunal of International Arbitration, Its Necessity and Value" 1 AJIL (1907) p. 342.

D.P. Meyers, "The Origin of the Hague Arbitral Courts" 8 AJIL (1914) p. 769.

M.O. Hudson, "The Permanent Court of Arbitration" 27 AJIL (1933) p. 440.

M.O. Hudson, "The Central American Court of Justice" 26 AJIL (1932) p. 759.

F.L. Grieves, *Supranationalism and International Adjudication* (Chicago: U. of ILL., 1969).

F. Boyle, "American Foreign Policy Toward International Law and Organizations 1898-1917" 6 Loyola of Los Angeles Int. and Comp. Law Jour. (1983) p. 185, pp. 292-307.

B.C.J. Loder, "The Permanent Court of International Justice and Compulsory Jurisdiction" II British Yearbook of Int. Law (1921-1922) p. 26.

Permanent Court of International Justice, The Hague, Publications 1922-1942.

U.N. General Assembly, International Law Commission, "Historical Survey of the Question of International Criminal Jurisdiction" (1949).

R. Jackson, *Report to the President*, June 6, 1945, International Conference on Military Trials (London: 1945).

R. Jackson, *The Case against the Nazi War Criminals* (N.Y.: Knopf, 1946)

B.V.A. Röling and C.F. Rüter, Eds. *The Tokyo Judgment* (Amsterdam: APA Univ. Press, 1977) 3 volumes.

S. Rosenne, *The Law and Practice of the International Court* (Leyden: Sijthoff, 1965) 2 volumes.

---

* AJIL abbreviates American Journal of International Law

R.D. Valentine, *The Court of Justice of the European Communities* (London: Stevens, 1965).

European Commission of Human Rights, Decisions and Reports, (Strasbourg, 1975-).

European Court of Human Rights, Publications, (Köln: Heymanns, 1961-).

Court of Justice of the European Communities, Digest of Cases (Luxemburg, 1981-).

A.J. Frowein, *"The European and the American Conventions on Human Rights — A Comparison"* 1 Human Rights Jour. (1980) p. 44.

T. Buergenthal, *"The Inter-American Court of Human Rights"* 76 AJIL (1982) p. 231.

Statutes of the Court of Justice of the Cartegena Agreement, XXIII Int. Legal Materials (Mar. 1984) p. 422.

L. Garber and C.M. O'Connor, *"The 1984 U.N. Sub-Commission on Prevention of Discrimination and Protection of Minorities"* 79 AJIL (1985) p. 168.

J. Schneider, *World Public Order of the Environment: Towards an Ecological Law and Organization* (Toronto: Univ. of Toronto, 1979).

R.B. Bilder, "The Settlement of Disputes in the Field of the International Law of the Environment" IV RdC* (1974) p. 145.

B.H. Oxman, "The Third U.N. Conference on the Law of the Sea" 75 AJIL (1981) p. 211, p. 243.

C. deVisscher, *Theory and Reality in Public International Law* (N.J.: Princeton Univ., 1968).

W.E. Darby, *International Tribunals* (London: Dent, 1904).

E. Wynner and G. Lloyd, *Searchlight on Peace Plans* (N.Y.: Dutton, 1949).

T. Marburg, *Development of the League of Nations Idea (N.Y.: Macmillan, 1932).*

D.H. Miller, *The Drafting of the Covenant* (N.Y.: Putnam, 1928).

F.P. Walters, *A History of the League of Nations* (London: Oxford Univ., 1952).

J.F. Green, "The Dumbarton Oaks Conversations" Dept. of State Bull. (1944) p. 459.

E. Borchard, "Criticism of the Dumbarton Oaks Proposals" 39 AJIL (1945) p. 97.

Report to the President on the Results of the San Francisco Conference, Dept. of State Publ. 2349 (Washington: USGPO, 1945) p. 67.

Ed. Comm., "The Central American Union" 7 AJIL (1913) p. 829.

Ed. Comm., "The Federation of Central America" 15 AJIL (1921) p. 255.

B. Turner, *The Other European Community, Integration and Cooperation in Nordic Europe* 1982).

R.J. Yalem, "Regionalism and World Order" 38 International Affairs (1962) p. 460.

P.C. Szasz, "The Law and Practices of the International Atomic Energy Agency" IAEC Series No. 7 (1970).

L.B. Sohn, "The Stockholm Declaration on the Human Environment" 14 Harv. Int. Law Jour. (1973) p. 423.

C.Q. Christol, *The Modern International Law of Outer Space* (N.Y.: Pergamon, 1982).

---

* RdC abbreviates *Recueil des Cours* (Collected courses of the Hague Academy of International Law).

J. Fried, "How Efficient is International Law" in K.W. Deutsch and S. Hoffman, Eds. *The Relevance of International Law* (Cambridge, Mass.: Schenckman, 1968) p. 93.

H. Nicolson, *The Congress of Vienna: A Study of Allied Unity 1812-1822* (N.Y.: Viking, 1961).

Documents on Disarmament, (Dept. of State 1945-   ).

A.H. Dean, *Test Ban and Disarmament* (N.Y.: Harper, 1966).

F.M. Auburn, *Antarctic Law and Politics* (Bloomington, Ind.: Indiana Univ., 1982).

A.G. Robles, "The Latin American Nuclear Weapons Free Zone" Occasional Paper 19, The Stanley Foundation, Muscatine, Iowa, (1979).

Sir Humphrey Milford, *International Sanctions* (London: Oxford Univ. 1939).

D.P. Meyers "Procedure for Applying Sanctions" 30 AJIL (1936) p. 124.

A.D. McNair, "Collective Security" 17 BYIL* (1936) p. 150.

J.F. Williams, "Sanctions Under the Covenant" 17 BYIL (1936) p. 130.

G. de Fiedorowicz, "Historical Survey of the Application of Sanctions" 22 Grotius Soc. (1937) p. 117.

S.D. Metzger, "Federal Regulation and Prohibition of Trade with Iron Curtain Countries" 29 Law and Contemp. Problems (1964) p. 1000.

R.L. Paarlberg, "Lessons of the Grain Embargo" Foreign Affairs, Fall, 1980, p. 144.

G. Ball, "The Case Against Sanctions" N.Y. Times Magazine, Sept. 12, 1982.

J.J. Paust, A. Blaustein and A. Higgins, *The Arab Oil Weapon* (Dobbs Ferry, N.Y.: Oceana, 1977).

D.W. Bowett, "Economic Coercion and Reprisal by States" 13 Virg. Jour. of Int. Law (1972) p. 1.

R. Higgins, *United Nations Peacekeeping, Documents and Commentary* London: Oxford Univ., 1981); 4 volumes.

O. Schachter, "Legal Aspects of the U.N. Action in the Congo" 55 AJIL (1961) p. 1.

O. Schachter, "The Evolving International Law of Development" 15 Col. Jou. of Trans. Law (1976) p. 1.

M. Bedjaoui, *Towards a New International Economic Order* (Paris: UNESCO, 1979).

K.S. Carlston, *Law and Organization in World Society* (Urbana: Univ. of Ill., 1962).

H. Lauterpacht, "The International Protection of Human Rights" I RdC (1947) p. 5.

J. Carey, *U.N. Protection of Civil and Political Rights* (N.Y. Syracuse Univ. 1970).

M. Moskowitz, *International Concern with Human Rights* (Leyden: Sitjhoff, 1974).

U.N. Yearbook on Human Rights, Annual.

M. McDougal, H.D. Lasswell and Lung-chu Chen, *Human Rights and World Public Order* (New Haven: Yale, 1980).

S.M. Schwebel, Ed. *The Effectiveness of International Decisions* (Leyden, Sijthoff, 1971).

M.S. McDougal and F.P. Feliciano, *Law and Minimum World Public Order* (New Haven: Yale, 1961).

Brownlie Ed. *Basic Documents on Human Rights* (Oxford: Clarendon, 1981).

---

* BYIL abbreviates British Yearbook of International Law

M. Moskowitz, *The Politics and Dynamics of Human Rights* (N.Y.: Oceana, 1968).

L.B. Sohn, and T. Buergenthal, Eds. *International Protection of Human Rights* (Indianapolis, Bobbs-Merrill, 1973).

PART TWO: WHAT *SHOULD* BE DONE

L. Henkin, "The Connally Reservation Revisited and, Hopefully, Contained" 65 AJIL (1971) p. 374.

C.W. Jenks, The *Prospects of International Adjudication* (London: Stevens, 1964).

M.C. Bassiouni and V.P. Nanda, *A Treatise on International Criminal Law* (Springfield, Ill.:, Thomas, 1973) 2 volumes.

R.A. Friedlander, *Terrorism, Documents of International and Local Control* (N.Y.: Oceana (1979))

L.B. Sohn, "The Role of Interntional Institutions as Conflict-Adjusting Agencies" 28 Univ. of Chicago Law Rev. (1961) p. 205.

G. Clark and L.B. Sohn, *World Peace Through World Law* (Cambridge, Mass.: Harvard Univ. 1958); later revised editions.

Campaign for U.N. Reform, *A Program to Reform and Restructure the U.N. System* (Wayne, N.J.: 1984).

World Association of World Federalists, *Proposals for Reform of the United Nations* (Chicago, Ill.: 1984).

R. Hudson, "The Case for the Binding Triad" Center for War/Peace Studies (N.Y.: 1983).

H. Stassen, *The Stassen Draft for a New United Nations* (Phila., Pa.: Glenview Fdtn. 1985).

B. Russell, *Common Sense and Nuclear Warfare* (N.Y.: Simon and Shuster 1959)

D.W. Bowett, "Economic Coercion and Reprisal by States" 13 Virginia Jour. of Int. Law (1972) p. 1.

M.P. Doxey, *Economic Sanctions and International Enforcement* (London: Macmillan, 1980).

PART THREE: WHAT *CAN* BE DONE

G.W. Ball, *The Discipline of Power* (Boston: Little Brown, 1968).

S. Melan, Ed. *Inspection for Disarmament* (N.Y.: Columbia Univ. 1958).

M. Krepon, "Arms Control; Verification and Compliance" No. 270, Headline Series, Foreign Policy Association (1984)

P.M. Mische, "Do the Soviets Cheat at Arms Controls?" The Whole Earth Papers, No. 21 (East Orange, N.J.: Global Ed. Associates, 1985).

T.M. Franck and E. Weisband, *Word Politics, Verbal Strategy Among the Superpower* (N.Y.: Oxford Univ., 1972).

F.A. Boyle, "International Lawlessness in the Caribbean Basin" 21-23 Crime and Social Justice (1984) p. 37.

J. Chace, *Endless War* (N.Y.: Vintage, 1984).

J. Korbel, *Detente in Europe, Real or Imaginary?* (Princeton N.J.: Princeton Univ., 1972)

S. Talbott, *Deadly Gambits, The Reagan Administration and the Stalemate in Nuclear Arms Control* (N.Y.: Knopf, 1984).

Common Security, A Blueprint for Survival, The Independent Commission on Disarmament and Security Issues (N.Y.: Simon and Shuster, 1982).

J. Carter, "Succeeding in the Arms Control Negotiations" N.Y. Times Magazine, May 12, 1985.

J. Stone, *Visions of World Order: Between State Power and Human Justice* (Baltimore, John Hopkins, 1984).

R. Falk, *The End of World Order* (N.Y.: Homes and Meier, 1983).

SUPPLEMENTARY BIBLIOGRAPHY

Anand, R.D. *Compulsory Jurisdiction of the International Court of Justice.* Bombay: Asia Press, 1961.

Bailey, Sidney D. *How Wars End: The United Nations and the Termination of Armed Conflict, 1946-1964.* NY: Clarendon Press, 1982.

Bassiouni, M. and Ved Nanda. *A Treatise on International Criminal Law.* 2 vols. IL: Charles C. Thomas Publishers, 1973.

Bebr, Gerhard. *Development of Judicial Control of the European Communities.* The Hague: Nijhoff, 1981.

Bernhardt, Rudolf, Ed., *Encyclopedia of Public International Law.* 12 vols. projected. Published under the auspices of the Max Planck Institute for Comparative Public Law and International Law. Amsterdam: North-Holland, 1981- .

Blacker, Coit D. and Duffy, Gloria. *International Arms Control: Issues and Agreements.* Stanford: Stanford University Press, 1984.

Boyle, Francis A. *World Politics and International Law.* Durham NC: Duke University Press, 1985.

Bowett, D.W. *The Law of International Institutions.* London: Stevens & Sons, 1975.

Brierly, James L. *The Law of Nations: An Introduction to the International Law of Peace.* Oxford: Clarendon Press, 1963.

Brownlie, Ian. *Principles of Public International Law.* Oxford: Clarendon Press, 1979.

Brownlie, Ian. *System of the Law of Nations: State Responsibility.* NY: Clarendon Press, 1983.

Corbett, Percy E. *The Growth of World Law.* NJ: Princeton University Press, 1971.

Court of Justice of the European Communities, *Digest of Case Law.* Luxembourg: 1981- .

Dhokalia, R.P. *The Codification of Public International Law.* Manchester: Manchester University Press, 1970.

Elias, Taslim O. *The International Court of Justice and Some Contemporary Problems: Essays in International Law.* The Hague: Nijhoff, 1983.

European Court of Human Rights, Publications. Strasbourg: 1961- .

Fisher, Roger and Urey, William. *Getting to Yes — Negotiating Agreements Without Giving In.* Boston: Harvard University Press, 1981.

Franck, Thomas M. *Human Rights in Third World Perspective.* 3 vols. NY: Oceana Publications, 1982.

Franck, Thomas M. *Nation Against Nation: What Happened to the U.N. Dream and What the U.S. Can Do About It.* NY: Oxford University Press, 1985.

Friedlander, Robert A. *Terrorism: Documents of International and Local Control.* 4 vols. NY: Oceana Publications, 1984.

Friedman, Leon, Ed. *The Law of War: A Documentary History.* 2 vols. NY: Randon House, Inc., 1972.

Friedmann, Wolfgang. *The Changing Structure of International Law.* NY: Columbia University Press, 1964.

Galtung, Johan. *There are Alternatives: Four Roads to Peace and Security.* PA: Dufour Editions, 1984.

Garcia-Amador, F.V. Ed. *The Inter-American System, Treaties, Conventions and Other Documents, an annotated compilation.* 4 vols. NY: Oceana Publications, 1983.

Gong, Gerrit W. *The Standard of 'Civilization' in International Society*. NY: Clarendon Press, 1984.

Gross, Leo. *Essays on International Law and Organization*. NY: Transnational Publishers, 1984.

Gross, Leo. *The Future of the International Court of Justice*. 2 vols. NY: Oceana Publications, 1976.

Haas, Michael, Ed. *Basic Documents of Asian Regional Organizations*. 8 vols. NY: Oceana Publications, 1979.

Hudson, Manley O. *International Tribunals Past and Future*. Washington, D.C.: Carnegie Endowment, 1944.

Humphrey, John P. *Human Rights and the United Nations: A Great Adventure*. NY: Transnational Publishers, 1984.

International Atomic Energy Agency, *International Treaties Relating to Nuclear Control and Disarmament*. Vienna: 1975.

International Court of Justice, *Yearbook*. Hague: 1947- .

Jacobson, Harold K. *Networks of Interdependence: International Organizations and the Global Political System*. NY: Alfred A. Knopf, 1984.

Jenks, Clarence W. *The Common Law of Mankind*. London: Stevens & Sons, 1958.

Joyner, Nancy D. *Aerial Hijacking as an International Crime*. NY: Oceana Publications, 1974.

Kim, Samuel S. *The Quest for a Just World Order*. Boulder, CO: Westview Press, 1984.

Kleckner, Simone-Marie. *Peaceful Settlement of Disputes in International Law: A Collection of Bibliographic and Research Sources*. NY: Oceana Publications, 1985.

Kleckner, Simone-Marie and Kudej, Blanka. *International Legal Bibliography*. NY: Oceana Publications, 1983.

Levie, Howard S. *The Code of International Armed Conflict*. 2 vols. NY: Oceana Publications, 1985.

Martin, Paul J. Ed., *Human Rights: A Topical Bibliography*. Boulder, CO: Westview Press, 1983.

Max Planck Institute for Comparative Public Law and International Law. "A current bibliography of articles." Published semi-annually. Berlin: 1975- .

McWhinney, Edward. *Conflict and Compromise: International Law and World Order in a Revolutionary Age*. NY: Homes & Meier Publishers, 1981.

Meron, Theodor (Ed.). *Human Rights in International Law: Legal and Policy Issues*. 2 vols. NY: Clarendon Press, 1984.

Meron, Theodor. *Human Rights Lawmaking in the United Nations*. Oxford: Oxford University Press, 1986.

Miller, Lynn H. *Global Order: Values and Power in International Politics* Boulder, CO: Westview Press, 1985.

Mische, Gerald and Patricia. *Toward a Human World Order*. NJ: Paulist Press, 1977.

Mosler, Hermann. *The International Society as a Legal Community*. Alphen: Sijthoff, 1980.

Murphy, John F. *The United Nations and the Control of International Violence: A Legal and Political Analysis*. NJ: Allanheld, Osmun & Co., 1982.

Noel-Baker, Philip J. *The Arms Race: A Program for World Disarmament*. NY: Oceana Publications, 1960.

Newcombe, Hanna. *Design for a Better World.* Washington DC: University Press, 1983.

Oellers-Frahm, Karin and Wühler, Norbert. *Dispute Settlement in Public International Law: Texts and Materials.* Berlin: Springer Verlag, 1984.

Pillar, Paul R. *Negotiating Peace: War Termination as a Bargaining Process.* NJ: Princeton University Press, 1983.

Robertson, A.H. *Human Rights in the World: An Introduction to the Study of the International Protection of Human Rights.* NY: St. Martin's Press, 1982.

Rosenne, Shabtai. *Practice and Methods of International Law.* NY: Oceana Publications, 1984.

Rosenne, Shabtai. *The World Court: What It Is and How It Works.* NY: Oceana Publications, 1974.

Sauvant, Karl P. *The Group of 77: Evolution, Structure, Organization.* NY: Oceana Publications, 1981.

Shore, William I. *Fact-Finding in Maintenance of International Peace.* NY: Oceana Publications, 1970.

Sohn, Louis B. *Basic Documents of African Regional Organizations.* 4 vols. NY: Oceana Publications, 1973.

Sohn, Louis B. and Gustafson, Kristen. *The Law of the Sea in a Nutshell.* St. Paul: West Publishing, Inc., 1984.

Stephenson, Carolyn M. Ed. *Alternative Methods for International Security.* Washington DC: University Press, 1982.

Stone, Julius, *Conflict Through Consensus: United Nations Approaches to Aggression.* Baltimore: John Hopkins University Press, 1977.

Szasz, Paul C. *The Law and Practices of the International Atomic Energy Agency.* Vienna: IAEA, 1970.

Szasz, Paul and others, *Convention on the Settlement of Investment Disputes between States and Nationals of Other States.* 2 vols. NY: Oceana Publications, 1970.

Thermat, Pieter VerLoren van. *The Changing Structure of International Economic Law.* The Hague: Nijhoff, 1981.

Trial of the Major War Criminals Before the International Military Tribunal. 42 vols. Nuremberg: 1949.

Trials of War Criminals Before the Nuremberg Military Tribunals Under Control Council Law No. 10. 15 vols. Washington DC: USGPO, 1953.

U.S. Arms Control and Disarmament Agency. *Agreements: Texts and Histories of Negotiations.* Washington DC: USGPO, 1982.

U.S. Department of the Army. *Treaties Governing Land Warfare.* Washington DC: USGPO, 1956.

Visscher, Charles de. *Theory and Reality in Public International Law* NJ: Princeton University Press, 1968.

Weston, Burns H. Ed. *Toward Nuclear Disarmament and Global Security: A Search for Alternatives.* Boulder CO: Westview Press, 1984.

Williams, Walter L. *Intergovernmental Military Forces and World Public Order.* NY: Oceana Publications, 1972.

Woito, Robert. *To End War: A New Approach to International Conflict.* NY: Pilgrim Press, 1982.

INDEX*

*References and Bibliography not included